STARTING & RU

B&B

IN

FRANCE

STARTING & RUNNING A

B&B

IN

FRANCE

*How to make money and enjoy a new lifestyle
running your own chambres d'hôtes*

DEBORAH HUNT

howto books

Cover photo is courtesy of Bed & Breakfast (France) who run the guide
'L'Association B&B France' and 'Bed & Breakfast Property Service'.
Contact www.bedbreak.com

Published by How To Books Ltd,
3 Newtec Place, Magdalen Road,
Oxford OX4 1RE, United Kingdom.
Tel: (01865) 793806. Fax: (01865) 248780.
email: info@howtobooks.co.uk
www.howtobooks.co.uk

Line drawings by Deborah Hunt

British Library Cataloguing in Publication Data
A catalogue record for this book is available from
the British Library

Cover design by Baseline Arts Ltd, Oxford
Produced for How To Books by Deer Park Productions
Typeset by TW Typesetting, Plymouth, Devon
Printed and bound by Bell & Bain Ltd., Glasgow

NOTE: The material contained in this book is set out in good faith for general guidance
and no liability can be accepted for loss or expense incurred as a result of relying in
particular circumstances on statements made in the book. Laws and regulations are
complex and liable to change, and readers should check the current position with the
relevant authorities before making personal arrangements.

The B&B shown on the cover is owned and run by Denyse Foucault in Vouillé which is
18km north west of Poitiers.

Dedication

This book is dedicated to my grand-daughter,
Francesca Viviana Teresa

Contents

Note from the Author

My aim in writing this book is to pass on my own experience of running a B&B in France for ten years, so that you too can run a successful and profitable business.

In a fast changing world where lifetime careers are no longer taken for granted, and early retirement is an increasing option, you could be looking for a different direction. If you want a challenge, then what better than to embark on a new job in another country? If you are truly looking for a complete change, if you have always wanted to run your own business, and are prepared for the hard work, then running a bed and breakfast could be for you. Just before we sold our B&B, I was asked by someone about to start if I thought it had been worth it. I said, 'It was bloody hard work, but it was great fun.' And it's the fun that keeps you going. You get far more out of living in France by joining the economy than by just living in a Brit enclave – and you meet some wonderful people of all nationalities.

In fact, there were two of us running the business: my husband and myself, but I seem to have taken on the job of writing up our experiences – with a lot of help of course. When we started, there didn't seem to be any help anywhere. We had to learn as we went along, making a few mistakes and feeling our way more slowly than we need have done. My intention is to speed your learning curve, give you confidence, and help with avoiding some of the pitfalls. It is primarily aimed at those new to living in France and who intend to run a more or less full time business, but I am sure that others will find many useful ideas. I have also assumed you intend to open the doors wide to all nationalities, although I accept that some British proprietors cater exclusively for their own compatriots. I have mostly used the UK as a basis for comparison with the way they do things in France, though with a few references to the USA where we lived for three years. We are both retired architects and so have been able to include chapters of advice on choosing and renovating suitable properties.

The wonderful thing about bed and breakfasts is their diversity. No two are alike and there is no one way to run your establishment. This book will give you plenty of ideas to set your imagination going.

Bonne chance!
Deborah Hunt

1

Before You Begin

Living in France has the following advantages for the British:

◆ The cuisine and lifestyle are highly regarded.
◆ It is our nearest foreign country.
◆ It is in the European Union.
◆ Property is cheaper.
◆ Best health service in the world.
◆ Less people per hectare and less vehicles per kilometre.
◆ Better climate (mostly).
◆ Many of us have already spent holidays there.

And disadvantages:

◆ Separation from family and friends.
◆ Life as an ex-pat can be difficult and frustrating at first.

- They speak French.
- Driving is a competitive sport.
- Baked beans/Cheddar cheese/Marmite are hard to find.

So much for living there. How about living there and running a B&B?
Advantages:

- No work permit needed (for EU residents).
- More tourist visitors than any other country in the world.

And disadvantages:

- *Taxe d'Habitation, Taxe Foncière, Taxe Professionelle, Taxe sur le Valeur Ajouté, Contributions Sociales, Assurance Vieillesse, Mutuelle, Impôt sur le Revenu.* (Each will be explained in Chapter 10.)

We found that the French were very reticent about giving out information. That is the opposite of the USA where they shower you with stuff. A French person explained that they think it impolite to give gratuitous information because it implies ignorance on the part of the listener. Of course they will always answer a direct question, but that supposes you know what questions to ask. So I shall be trying to forestall as many questions as possible.

LIVING THE DREAM

By now you will have made up your mind about living in France. Moving to another country after a career in the UK has become so popular it has even acquired the name 'living the dream'. You come for the laid-back lifestyle in a better climate, the cheaper property, and to get away from the stress of the 12-hour a day job with suits, meetings and sales targets. Unfortunately, some people have to earn a living. The most popular choice for foreigners is the leisure industry. For one thing, a formal training isn't essential, and for another we British have the next best language to speak after French, given that you're living in France. You will be in good company. Tony Blair worked as a barman in Paris before taking another job; that's how he comes to speak French. However, you have got to cope with a new country, a new language and a new job, all at once; and it can be daunting.

If the choice is to run a Bed & Breakfast I will help you to:

◆ Choose the property.
◆ Adapt or restore it.
◆ Make the business profitable.
◆ Avoid the pitfalls.
◆ Cope with the formalities.
◆ Advertise effectively.
◆ Make your guests recommend you and come back again.

WHAT IS A BED & BREAKFAST?

The word 'hotel' is universal, but there are many names for staying as a paying guest in a private house or very small establishment. In English-speaking countries, it's 'bed and breakfast' or 'guest house' or 'inn'. In French-speaking countries, it's *chambres d'hôtes*. Not only does the name differ, but the concept does too. Since so much of French life revolves around the table, it's not surprising to find that many such establishments serve meals, and it is the only country with a name for this presentation, which is *table d'hôte*.

The well known formula of B&B was pioneered in Britain over 100 years ago, originally mostly in seaside resorts. France doesn't have this tradition. For inexpensive lodgings there were only *pensions* or the cheaper hotels. *Pensions* were more than a B&B because they always served meals, but less than a hotel with its restaurant service, and they were always in noisy town centres. With their antiquated plumbing and rock-hard bolsters, they have gone now. The era of the car means we don't have to stay in town centres any more, and the second half of the twentieth century brought in the concept of *chambres d'hôtes*. These are always in the country or in villages, and are seldom accessible by public transport. A *chambres d'hôtes* can be as small as one bedroom and serving only breakfast, up to a *château* with every luxury and serving gourmet meals. The maximum number of guests is fifteen, and meals can only be served to resident guests. In the UK, the smaller of these establishments would be called a 'B&B', and the larger a 'guest house'.

The B&B concept has increased enormously in the past few years; some departments have seen the number triple in the past decade. Fortunately, there are many more customers, both because we take more trips and because the big chain hotels become ever more bland.

QUALIFICATIONS

There are only two: an ability to work hard, and an ability to speak French. You will already know your capacity for hard work. If you do not already speak French it has **got** to be learned **now**. You should be going to classes before leaving the UK, and they should lead to a formal examination. See 'Hotcourses' under 'Addresses' for details of what is available near you. For beginners, the GCSE is good. But don't take A-level because it has too much emphasis on literature. Running a B&B requires different skills from those needed to appreciate the great French writers. Many new arrivals think they will absorb the language in a year just by being here. Alas, they won't; it takes more application than that. Courses leading to the Institute of Linguistics exam or the Open University are best (see Appendix for addresses). A new Open University course 'Bon Départ: Beginners French' starts in November 2004 and will have on-line or face to face tutorials. For those whose O- and A-level French were a long time ago, it is a matter of recapturing that standard, and classes will be better than doing it alone. I'm not saying you have to be fluent, but you need to be able to cope with a wide variety of situations. There are total immersion residential courses, but they are expensive and the money would be better spent on the business. My one caveat on language courses is: if you plan to do dinners, should one of you go to a short professional cookery course?

THE REWARDS

You'll be working seven days a week in July and August, and long days at that if you do dinners. The 35-hour week does not apply to the self-employed. However, there is no travelling, and for most of the rest of the year you can work at your own pace. Even though you may drive yourself hard, it is still less stressful than working for someone else. It has to be said that you don't make much money in the first few years, possibly even a loss at first. But by the third or fourth year the business should be established and you should be making some profit. Providing, that is, you haven't taken on too much, have chosen the property carefully, and kept a tight control of the expenses.

ONE OR TWO BEDROOMS

The income will be small, so you must be doing it to supplement another source. Really it can hardly fail to pay **provided** you don't spend too much on improvements or advertising. It will pay because otherwise the rooms will presumably just be standing empty except when there are friends or relatives visiting. When it's paying guests the extra expenses will hardly be noticed.

Improvements

After adding a bathroom to each bedroom, **do not** spend too much. Since the bathrooms will increase the value of the house, you don't need to attribute all the cost to the miniature B&B business. Though if it proves exceptionally expensive to add two bathrooms, and the rooms have to share, this may be the best option. In this case both rooms can only be let to one family at a time. The paying guests **should not** share a bathroom with the hosts. In a two-storey house you could devote the first floor to the guests, and if it's empty in the winter there's no need for heating. It **will not** pay to put a swimming pool in just for the visitors; but if you want one anyway, here is a wonderful chance to help pay for it.

Dinner

If you offer dinners at all, you could make it only once a week – say on arrival or Saturdays. You want to get to know people if they are staying *en famille*, as the French would say, but it would be very onerous to do it every night.

Advantages

- Low capital expenditure.
- Easy to discontinue the business.
- Can pick and choose the guests.
- Bedrooms available for own family and friends when required.
- Avoids the loneliness of living in an isolated property.

Disadvantages
◆ Low income.
◆ Loss of privacy.

THREE OR FOUR BEDROOMS

This number of rooms gives a great variety of establishments:

1. It could be a reasonable business in its own right.

2. It could be part of the development plan for something larger.

3. If some of the bedrooms are a suite of two rooms then it does form a larger enterprise and could hold 10–12 guests.

The *chambres d'hôtes* organisations class a suite as one room, and it is a very useful arrangement. A children's room can be entered via the main bedroom (and locked when not in use), or it could be a mezzanine, and both share the bathroom. 3 or 4 bedrooms will not produce a living but will be a substantial addition to another income.

Improvements
I assume you have a house with at least 4 or 5 bedrooms and 2 or 3 reception rooms. I trust the house and services are in reasonable condition, because the scale of the business will not pay for a major restoration. Maybe you wanted to restore the property anyway and are only looking to the B&B to help out. Otherwise, as before, adding extra bathrooms is the major expense.

Dinner
This can depend on how much you like cooking because it will not be on a scale to make a big difference to the income. If there are restaurants nearby it's optional, but if you are isolated then it's essential.

Advantages
◆ Moderate capital expenditure.
◆ Can be run by one person, or a retired couple.
◆ Doesn't need too large a house.
◆ Justifies some cleaning help.

Disadvantages
- ◆ Does not produce enough income for a couple to live on.
- ◆ Loss of privacy.
- ◆ Needs to be well advertised, but cost not always justified by results.

FIVE OR SIX BEDROOMS

This is a serious business and to make a success of it you will need real business acumen. To make a reasonable living for two people, you will need one or more of the following:

1. *Table d'hôte*, possibly with full drinks licence.
2. Open all year in a location where this will be effective.
3. Have some other activity such as self catering *gîtes*, or classes or a sport.

It will be a full time occupation and will need some paid help if there are only two of you and you do dinners. If more than two partners you will have to promote the business really extensively.

Advantages
- ◆ Can produce a good income.
- ◆ Justifies cleaning, or catering, or gardening help.
- ◆ Justifies the privacy of own separate accommodation.
- ◆ Good use for a large property.
- ◆ Great job satisfaction in having created a viable business.

Disadvantages
- ◆ Large capital expenditure.
- ◆ Long hours, 7 days a week in high season.
- ◆ Dinner for more than 10 every day difficult without experience.
- ◆ 6 bedrooms incurs the expense of fire regulations.
- ◆ If you have a large garden with a pool and you offer a complete holiday experience with full board, then a couple **cannot** manage this on their own.

GITES DE FRANCE AND CLEVACANCES

These are two separate government-run organisations, and you can join one of them if you wish. It is not compulsory. Both have *chambres d'hôtes* proprietors as well as *gîte* members. Both operate a grading scheme of 4 levels and you need to be at the 3rd or 4th level for the international market. Grade 3 includes the great majority of B&Bs; grade 4 requires a building of special character and a near professional standard of presentation. Both are somewhat similar to the English Tourist Board (or its equivalents), and they produce brochures and are agents for the government grants for renovation.

Gîtes de France

This was founded in 1954 jointly by the ministry of agriculture and the ministry of tourism to promote farm dwellings as holiday *gîtes* because so many of the original population had left the countryside due to the mechanisation of farming. It gave an extra source of income to farmers and a boost to tourism. In short it was a winner all round and the word *gîte* has entered the English language. In 1969 they added *chambres d'hôtes* to an already established brand with a well-known logo. While the concept has taken a firm hold, unfortunately the name has not had the same impact, and the English words 'bed and breakfast' are widely recognised in France. Their grading scheme is 1 to 4 *épis* (ears of corn). The maximum number of bedrooms is mostly 6, in a few *départements* it is 5 and in some others 6 only if one room is for the disabled. See Chapter 12 for further details.

Clévacances

This was founded in 1995. The government wanted to bring all *chambres d'hôtes* and *gîte* owners into a recognised organisation so that they could be inspected and graded, with the aim of improving standards. *Clévacances* only allows a maximum of 5 bedrooms. Their grading scheme is 1 to 4 *clés* (keys). See Chapter 12 for further details.

WHO RUNS A B&B?

Normally it is a couple or other family group. I assume you know each other well enough to assess whether you will make a good team. Setting up in business with friends is a different matter. Do be very cautious because there is a saying that it is easier to get divorced than to break a business partnership. At the very least take a holiday together to see if you get on. Before you even begin, make a formal agreement on the terms for breaking up. How many partners are there going to be in this enterprise? If it is more than two, then even a large B&B on its own is unlikely to produce enough income.

There has been a change in the age group moving to France recently. At first it was mostly retired people. Now it attracts many younger people who can afford the move due to the high property prices in the UK, but they still need a steady income for many years yet. Either they must work very hard at the B&B business or must have another income.

How old are you? Sorry to ask such an impertinent question. Just letting a spare bedroom or two will be quite feasible into your eighties provided you can manage the stairs. But a serious business requires such a big capital investment that it really needs a ten-year run to get a return. Possibly you have taken early retirement, in which case project forward to see if you think you will still be fit enough or have the energy for the work. Older people do have one advantage:— their pensions will soon arrive or perhaps already have. This will smooth over any rough patches. Younger people have the energy but need a steady income for many years yet. Either they must work very hard at the B&B business or they must have an additional source of income.

Paradoxically running a B&B is ideal for shy people. You meet many guests you would be far too timid to approach socially.

A BALANCED BUSINESS

The most common cause of failure is taking on too much: too big a house or too grandiose a scheme. The French are amazed at the scale of some of the crazy ideas these foreigners have. They are grateful of course for the amount of money we lavish on some of their ruins. In fact do not do in France something you would not dream of doing at home. Be prudent, do not borrow too much, and always reckon that whatever you are doing will overspend. Budget that there will be no profit at all at first if you are doing building work and precious little in the early years if you are starting the business from scratch. It will take three to five years to build the business up and even then there can be bad years through no fault of your own. There are national and international events that seriously damage the tourist trade, or disaster can strike you personally. So always keep a reserve.

Starting right in with the maximum number of bedrooms intended is the truly commercial way. You build the business up quickly and get a proper return on the money spent as soon as possible. It is a great incentive to **have** to fill all those rooms. But if you lack experience, are short of funds, or are nervous about putting so much money into the venture; then you may prefer to proceed cautiously. You could start with 2 bedrooms, and add further facilities and another bedroom each year. In this case you **must** set a limit, say 5 years, by which to have finished the improvements and not spend any more. If you keep on dabbling right up to the time you give up or sell, you won't have had a full return on the investment.

PLANNING THE MOVE

It is not the French way to buy and sell property on the same day, though it can be done. Nor would I like to be involved in the complexities of selling in one country and buying in another on the same day. Unless you have the capital, it is best to sell in the UK first. You then know exactly how much you have made, and, with it earning interest, you can afford to rent until you are established in France. The furniture can be stored with a firm that does international removals, and you can take your time for a thorough house search.

Possibly you are considering keeping your former home and letting it, or buying a smaller one as a pad. Realistically I do not think you will have the time, and you will lose bookings by being absent from the B&B for long periods. Also, whichever house you are not in needs looking after.

The property search can begin before you go to France:

1. Search the internet.
2. Go to the French property exhibition.
3. Read the 'French Property News'.

For details of the last two see under 'French Property News' in 'Addresses'. Then, for a serious search, the best way is to hire a *gîte* for a month or more in the winter. Find names in the holiday brochures and see what offers you can get for a long winter let, not forgetting to check that there is central heating. If the owners are British and resident on site, so much the better, as they will be a fund of local knowledge and can give tips on buying in France arising from their own recent experience.

You must also engage in some industrial espionage, by which I mean staying the night in at least 6 other B&Bs. You will learn a lot and begin to form your own opinions about how to run your own place. It will give a great feeling of superiority because of course you will also decide to do it better.

TIPS TO MAKE IT PAY

- Decide on the size of the business and do not take on too much.
- Do plenty of preliminary research.
- Be absolutely sure all the partners form a good team.

TIP FOR LEARNING FRENCH

- Classes with a formal exam produce the best result.

2

Choosing the Property

THE QUICK WAY IN

Have you thought of buying a B&B as a going concern? Here are the advantages:

1. You can move in, take two weeks to settle down, and start making money in week three.

2. All costs are known in advance.

3. There should be plenty of advice from the previous owners.

4. You can probably buy the contents (furniture, curtains, linen, tableware) very reasonably.

5. It can take five years to build up a business; you are coming into one already established.

6. You get the benefit of all the advertising in previous years.

7. You can examine the previous year's accounts.

Here are the disadvantages:

1. The building may not be as sound as it looks and the DIY may be badly done.

2. The services may be poor.

3. If you do not speak French you will find life very difficult.

4. You are taking on the reputation of the previous owners.

5. You are stuck with the previous owners' taste.

6. Due to limited supply, there will be little choice of region.

7. You may want to run it differently, so there will be little benefit from buying a going concern.

Think about it seriously. I see the main advantage being that you can start earning straight away. If you have **got** to earn a living this is important. But you would have to make sure the previous owners had taken firm advance bookings, that the clients have all been informed of the change of ownership, and if a deposit has been paid you would have to keep to the same prices.

The dream of converting an old property which you have bought cheaply is seductive, but it can take years for the building work, and more years to build up the business. While it is important to look at the last year's accounts, they may not tell you much. Some people about to sell have let the place run down, particularly if the owners are getting divorced or there is some other family problem. The place may be looking a bit tired or there may be scope for increasing the prices and for advertising more effectively. Have an accountant look at the figures. He'll need to be bilingual if they are in French. He must then advise whether the business could make a living, taking into account any mortgage and the projected income.

A *chambres d'hôtes* with 4 or more bedrooms and in reasonable condition will cost **at least** £200,000 (2003 prices), possibly a lot more depending on size, location and the amount of land. Any goodwill element can be expected to be included in the asking price, but check this. If the owner will not come below the asking price, you may be able to negotiate to include the furniture. But check that it's worth having. With several bedrooms, the value of the second-hand contents is about £10,000 or more depending on quality. It would cost a lot more than this to buy it all new. Make quite sure you have a detailed inventory.

You should be able to pick up most of the business that the previous owners were generating. Don't close for too long, and don't let the business die away even if you are planning to make changes later on.

A lack of French may be the biggest hurdle in taking over a going concern. It would be slightly easier to start in the winter with less customers around. You would certainly have severe difficulties with several bedrooms and starting in high season, unless you have hotel experience. Regrettably some business does drop away when new proprietors take over. Many previously faithful clients will not come again to new owners, especially if of a different nationality, and the locals will not come until they've had time to size you up. Advertising entries have to be in by the previous autumn and this may not have been done. *Gîtes de France* and *Clévacances* memberships are not transferable, and they do not accept new members until after the bedrooms have been inspected fully furnished. Then you only get into the following year's guide. All these situations should be discussed with the vendors to see if any help can be provided.

CHOOSING FOR YOUR OWN LIFESTYLE

The big decision you will already have made is whether this adventure is to be a small sideline of letting a couple of bedrooms in what is 90 per cent your own home, or a serious business occupying 90 per cent of the property with yourselves in the remaining small corner. If you are also planning to have several *gîtes*, *ferme auberge* (restaurant), riding stable, etc. then you're going into business in a big way and need more advice than I can give. Please do take advice. **Do not** get carried away by the fact that property is cheap.

There are two main things to consider in choosing a location. One is what is best for the business. The other is that you will be living there all year long.

Let's consider yourself first. If you think you will need to pop back to the UK frequently, it means either the north west or near a suitable airport. The trouble with the new regional airports is that the services change with great rapidity.

Have you visited your favourite holiday area in the winter? Everyone loves Provence. Well, actually, not in winter. Most of the restaurants and shops close down, the mistral blows and it has a very dead feel out of season. Anyway, property is twice the price. It's a super spot for business though.

If you isolate yourself deep in the country, do you think you can cope if you are not used to rural living? You may be lonely in the winter and it's no fun being snowed in. And if one of you may need to work, remember there's very little employment in the remote areas; that's why the young people have left and property is cheap. If you have children, you will want to investigate schools. For the state school it's obligatory to go to the one in the catchment area in which you live. If you choose somewhere that's popular with foreigners, you mustn't be surprised to find that most are retired and may not be your age group. But you'll be joining them one day and may like to stay in an area where you have made many friends.

CHOOSING THE RIGHT LOCATION FOR THE BUSINESS

If you're going to build the business up from scratch, choosing the location is one of the most important decisions you'll make. Look first at where the professionals are. You come off a motorway junction and there are four hotels in a row. Go to the remote countryside and there is no hotel within thirty miles. I'm not suggesting you should be alongside a motorway slip road, but the moral is that you have got to go to the people, they don't come to you. You'll be surprised at this because you thought the remote farmstead was just the thing, and it's cheap, too. The busiest B&B I've seen was on the outskirts of Paris and 3 kilometres from Disneyland. The proprietor said they were 'a bit quiet in January'. I didn't like to admit we were a bit quiet in November, December, January, February and March.

Once you've selected a property, you should check with the tourist office to see if there are any other B&Bs nearby. This is not necessarily a bad thing as you can pass on guests to each other when full, but that's difficult if the prices are very different.

IN A VILLAGE

In my opinion B&Bs are too few in some of the most picturesque villages in the world. There are many advantages. You don't have to provide dinners as there will be restaurants nearby. You will be near a baker for the fresh bread and croissants, and near most of the other support services you need. There will be only a small garden if any at all. In fact a very manageable business. However, the downside is the lack of parking. Maybe you can find something not too far away.

There are 144 villages classified by the government as '*Les Plus Beaux Villages de France*'. No chain hotels here with their neon signs, but very suitable for a B&B if you don't mind being told exactly what you can do with the exterior of your property. There are even a few without a single *chambres d'hôtes*. See Appendix A for the list of villages. But there are many more delightful villages not quite in the first rank.

This is **the best** choice for an all-year business. Most stays will be for 1 night, a few will be for 2 or 3. *Gîtes de France*'s official definition of a village is maximum 2,000 population, but most branches are a bit more flexible.

NEAR A MAIN ROAD

Of course you can't advertise on an *autoroute* (motorway), but your brochure could stress that you are not far from a junction. This works better in the north for all those Europeans making the long journey south.

Not everyone rushes along motorways. The *Routes Nationales* ('A' roads) still carry plenty of traffic and you can have a sign actually on the roadside.

Have you heard of the '*bis*' roads? You are a real Francophile if you know that '*bis*' is short for *bison futé* (literally: cunning buffalo). They are government designated alternatives to the main roads and are for drivers who want to enjoy the scenery. Just the people you are after. There is a free map available at motorway service areas and some garages and tourist offices. In the country of the *Tour de France* you could make a pitch for cyclists too by advertising in their specialist magazines.

You need to be far enough from the road for noise not to be a problem, but not so far that people get lost. You really should do dinners as travellers don't want to go out again. The clientele will be all one night stays, and the nearer the channel ports or tunnel you are, the longer the season will be.

SEA, COUNTRY, MOUNTAIN

See Chapter 8 for figures on the big difference in occupancy rates between a country location and a village centre. Don't kid yourself that you will be able to fill all the rooms for most of the year in a remote area.

These scenic locations are for the longer stay holiday, though you'll still get a few single-night customers. You'll have to offer dinners and give some thought to what clients are going to do for lunches even if you don't provide them yourself.

At the sea you'll want to make a big pitch for children. If you've said 'near' the sea, don't be too far away – no one likes that. There is no need to provide much in the way of facilities unless you wish, but an indoor heated pool would be a real winner for those occasional cold wet summer days.

The French have a deep attachment to their countryside and a working farm or former farm is very popular. Other nationalities too love an old farmhouse in the country. If it's not a working farm and not by the sea, and you want long stay visitors, then you really should have a swimming pool and try to provide as many other activities as possible. There may be very little in the vicinity.

In the mountains there may be skiing which gives a winter season. And you'll get a summer season too, especially individualists who appreciate the scenery, the air and the tranquillity. I saw one B&B in such a location that advertised 'no TV, no radio, no traffic'. Quite so.

The main disadvantage of most of these situations is the short season. There is a big capital investment all for four months of the year, and even then you are not likely to be full in June and September. If there's a sporting activity you're keen on yourself, perhaps you could incorporate it in your holiday promotion: sailing, canoeing, riding and fishing come to mind. There is an extensive network of *grandes randonnées* (hiking trails) and although some hikers consider B&Bs too frilly you might catch some if you are well placed.

NEAR A TOURIST ATTRACTION

France has more world class historic sites classified by UNESCO than any other country (*see Fig. 1*). Most are in towns but you don't have to be right alongside to list it as a local attraction; being nearby will do very well. For

---

Chartres Cathedral
Decorated Grottoes of the Vézère Valley
Mont-St Michel and its Bay
Palace and Park of Versailles
Vézelay, Church and Hill
Amiens Cathedral
Cistercian Abbey of Fontenay
Palace and Park of Fontainebleau
Roman and Romanesque Monuments of Arles
Roman Theatre and its Surroundings and the 'Triumphal Arch' of Orange
Royal Saltworks of Arc-et-Senans
Place Stanislas, Place de la Carrière, and Place d'Alliance in Nancy
Church of Saint-Savin-sur-Gartempe
Cape Girolata, Cape Porto, Scandola Nature Reserve and the Piano Calanches in Corsica
Pont du Gard (Roman Aqueduct)
Strasbourg, Grand Ile
Paris, Banks of the Seine
Cathedral of Notre-Dame, Former Abbey of Saint-Rémi and Palace of Tau, Reims
Bourges Cathedral
Historic Centre of Avignon
Canal du Midi
Historic Fortified City of Carcassonne
Historic Site of Lyon
Routes of Santiago de Compostela in France
Jurisdiction of Saint-Emilion, Gironde
The Loire Valley between Sully-sur-Loire and Chalonnes-sur-Loire
Provins, Town of Medieval Fairs

Figure 1   UNESCO World heritage sites

example a B&B near Chartres attracts a lot of Americans. Most tourists from the other side of the world don't stray much from the well-beaten track, but there are thousands of years of history from which to make a choice, from cave paintings to World War II; all have left their mark. Choose the location, read it up, and advertise. You should have a fairly long season, but one night stays only.

TOWNS

No, **not in** them, but in the countryside just outside. You'll not get the international tourists but there will be a large local population with all their friends and relatives. The French visit a lot: there are weddings, funerals, first communions, golden weddings, to name only a few of the excuses for getting the family together. It's a big country so they often have to come a long way and need to stay. There'd be people house hunting, coming to local events, all sorts of reasons. There will be just a few on business. This is the only way you could be in some of the more industrial areas. There are usually some pleasant pockets in what used to be village centres. You should seriously consider doing dinners because that is the point – you are offering something more homely than a hotel. You'll need to get *Gîtes de France* to approve the location before you buy because you'll want French customers and it would be a blow if they decided it was not rural enough.

It may be that one of you is working in a big city. This doesn't rule out the other partner running a B&B just outside as described above.

WHERE TO AVOID

It may seem as if most of France is a desirable location. **Not so**. The centre of towns and cities are **out**. For one thing *Gîtes de France* won't accept you, for another I wouldn't want yobs knocking on the door late at night. Nor will *Gîtes de France* accept a house on a *lotissement* (housing estate). It's a great disadvantage when the surroundings are unprepossessing, even when the welcome is warm. I stayed in a B&B where the countryside was totally flat and all you could see were electricity pylons in every direction. The B&B wasn't so great either, or was I prejudiced? I would avoid Corsica while it's politically unstable.

THE HOUSE

It's a difficult choice because there are types of house quite unknown in the UK. To start with the best: the *4 épis/clés* category requires a building with some architectural merit, or an exceptionally high standard of presentation. Even after restoration, the maintenance costs of a large old property will be enormous and the heating costs outrageous. A B&B business will only help towards the upkeep. An illustration of the scale of the problem is that I heard of a mansion sold for the equivalent of £1; in other words it was given away. Please do be **very cautious**.

For the *3 épis/clés* category the choice is wide. It could be a modern house which will be a great saving on the upkeep, but most of us foreigners prefer something old with plenty of character. If this is to be a profitable venture **do not** take on too much. An ordinary-sized house will generally be large enough for the guest bedrooms, kitchen, dining room, possibly a lounge, and accommodation for yourselves. In old farm houses you need to be aware that the ground floor was originally for the animals; the humans lived on the first floor. This means that the ground floor is low. For town houses, though they may look like 3 storeys from the road, they are often 5 storeys with a semi-basement and rooms in the roof space. A view is always a good advertising point.

Be imaginative. Could you buy two houses next door to each other, one for yourselves, and one for the guests? Or perhaps one across the road? Quirky premises are a real attention grabber too. I've seen pictures of a B&B on a barge, in a *pigeonnier* (dove cote), and in a gipsy caravan. Brilliant.

What the house does need is a prettiness factor for the publicity photo call: thatch, half-timbering, mellow stone, mature trees, courtyard and water are all winners. Squint through the camera lens and imagine how it will look in a 2 × 3cm-size photo in a guidebook. This, more than anything else, is what grabs the customers' attention as they flip through. Perhaps it could be improved with some creeper here and some demolition there. It sounds cynical, but your future income is at stake.

THE LAND

The opposite situation to the house. Don't be afraid of buying all that is offered. Land is cheap in France (except in towns) and it will be a good selling point one day.

A few cautions:

1. Steeply sloping gardens make access difficult and swimming pools more expensive.

2. If agricultural land is already let, you will not be able to get possession.

3. Don't take planning permission for granted.

4. Check out the commercial neighbours for noise.

5. Is there enough room for all the parking you will need?

6. Check that there is mains drainage not too far from the building or that you can get permission for a septic tank.

7. Check that telephone, electricity and water are available if not already existing.

balcon (m)	balcony	maison à étage (f)	2 storey house
bastide (f)	medieval village	maison de maître	master's house
bergerie (f)	sheepfold	manoir (m)	manor
château (m)	castle, mansion	mas (m)	Provence farmhouse
chaumière (f)	cottage	moulin à eau (m)	water mill
demeure (f)	home	moulin à vent	wind mill
ferme (f)	farm, farmhouse	pièce (f)	room
ferme en activitée	working farm	plan d'eau (m)	leisure lake
gentilhommière (f)	gentleman's house	randonnée (f)	hiking trail
lotissement (m)	housing estate	village perché (m)	hill town

Figure 2   Glossary

TIPS FOR MAKING IT PAY

◆ Choose location very carefully.
◆ Do not buy too large a property.

- ◆ Do buy all the land.
- ◆ Do not be too isolated if you are not used to country self sufficiency.

TIP FOR IMPROVING YOUR FRENCH

- ◆ Speak only French at meal times.

3

Buying Your Property

PEOPLE YOU ARE LIKELY TO MEET

Acheteur	Buyer (i.e. yourself)
Agent immobilier	Estate agent
Architecte	Architect
Entrepreneur	Building contractor
Expert immobilier	Buildings surveyor
Géomètre	Land surveyor
Notaire	Notary
Secrétaire	Secretary (of any of these)
Vendeur	Vendor

A DIFFERENT SYSTEM

You must not believe that buying in France is easy and straightforward, but nor must you think it is impossibly difficult. Understanding the system will allow you to plan ahead and proceed with more confidence. France has evolved a good and workable method for property purchase which cuts out most of the uncertainty experienced in the UK. The *notaire* does not perform exactly the same functions as does a solicitor in the UK. Because he acts for both parties, there is less aggravation, and since a preliminary contract is signed immediately an offer is accepted, there is almost no gazumping. It is not noticeably quicker, but when moving house, speed is not of the essence, it is certainty that matters. The French move house less frequently than we do in the UK and property is still often passed down the generations, so one's home is not seen as an investment opportunity on which to make fat profits. This makes property prices far more stable, though they have been rising since the mid-nineties.

ESTATE AGENT

This is a new breed in France. Traditionally, property purchase was negotiated by a *notaire* and they still handle many, but nowadays more than 50 per cent are done through estate agents as we know them. All agents based in the UK will be working in association with a French agent, but there are some British agents based only in France. Your first contacts will probably be with British agents, but once you have arrived in France call in on any local agents you see in your chosen area. Every small town has at least one. They may not be geared particularly towards foreigners, but they will have a lot of detailed local knowledge and will produce someone who speaks English if necessary. Agents' fees are not regulated, but are normally 5 per cent and are usually paid by the purchaser. In this case it will be included (and hidden) in the sale price, but check this; especially if you have negotiated the price down. Don't believe a word they say about renovation costs; get your own estimates.

MAKING AN OFFER

Sole agencies are rare, so agents are in cut-throat competition with each other. Addresses of properties are not divulged and agents always take you there personally. You would probably never find them by yourself anyway as there are no road names in the countryside. You will have to sign that you saw the property first with them. This is so you cannot do a private deal or buy through another agent. It is a myth that there is one price for the locals and one for foreigners, the difference is that the French will bargain harder.

The time to pause is when you have seen a suitable property. If you make an offer that is accepted, the agent will try to rush you to the *notaire* at the earliest possible moment. You will sign up with only a minimum of escape clauses, and certainly no survey or estimate of any work required. It is in the agent's interest to rush you because a delay means another could get in first and he would lose the sale. Without sole agencies there are no 'gentlemen's agreements' about not continuing to market a house under offer. This works the other way too of course, in that you could lose the property if you haven't signed. On balance it's best to be cautious and, anyway, always make an offer. We lost a very pretty property while we were thinking about it and I was very upset at the time. Since we eventually found an even better one it was for the best in the end. There are some bargains at auctions of repossessed properties, but don't attempt this unless you speak fluent French.

SURVEYOR

In France it is not the custom to have a survey before buying property. In the UK we mostly do. Here lies a problem, because British people arriving in France therefore expect a survey to be an element of the buying process. Since French mortgages are from banks, a survey forms no part of the negotiations; the bank is only interested in your ability to pay the monthly charge. If the mortgage is from a British institution, then a survey may be required. An adverse report would give you some facts to help in negotiating the price downwards, but since the French bargain hard anyway, this is only a slight advantage.

So a survey has one function only which is to help you make the decision on whether to buy. If the survey is to be made after you have signed, then you could have a *clause suspensive* (condition) included in the document to the effect that it is subject to a satisfactory survey. This is unusual and the vendor may refuse. If the clause has gone in, then you might be able to reach a compromise on the price. Ask the estate agent for a name because a French person will know the local construction better.

ARCHITECT

If the house is in poor condition or you envisage doing a lot of work, then you need an architect. He will advise on the structure and also give a preliminary estimate of the cost of the work proposed. Most people think first of asking a builder for an estimate. However, without some drawings you are unlikely to be able to supply enough information for him to give anything like an accurate price. Converting an ordinary house or farm outbuildings into a mini-hotel is a complex operation. Using an architect is worthwhile even when you plan to do all the work yourself. Ask the agent for a name. There are even a few British architects practising in France.

NOTARY *(Notaire)*

This a prestigious occupation and he (or she) should be addressed as '*Maître X*'. You will have been surprised that the one *notaire* acts for both buyer and seller. Or rather the truth is he doesn't 'act' for either. He is an impartial professional whose functions are to collect the taxes, establish the correct owner, pay any mortgages, and deal with the conveyancing process. Thus he is on neither 'side'. You must accept that he is re-active and not pro-active, which means that he will obey instructions but will not give opinions. He will only do searches to ascertain anything affecting the property directly. For anything affecting the property indirectly such as new roads, high tension power cables, etc., you have to do your own research at the *Direction Départemental de l'Equipement/DDE* (works department) for your commune.

You can appoint your own *notaire* and the cost will be the same as they split the fee, but there is really no advantage. The *notaire*'s fees and the taxes will be 10–15 per cent of the purchase price, which is considerably more than in the UK. If the *notaire*'s office is near your property, it is a good idea to meet him at least once in the process; he may be a very useful contact in the future. However, they rarely speak English.

For finding property for sale by *notaires* go to their own web site:
   www.immonot.com

If a *notaire* is the selling agent, then this is the one time when it would be best to appoint someone else yourself.

PRELIMINARY CONTRACT *(Compromis de vente)*

Your offer has been accepted and in the UK you never see the estate agent again. In France the agent will stay with you right through to completion. Discuss with him any *clauses suspensives* (conditions) you want to include in the preliminary contract.

Some possible conditional clauses:

◆ Obtaining a mortgage.
◆ A satisfactory survey.
◆ Selling a previous house.
◆ Obtaining a *certificat d'urbanisme* (preliminary planning permission).
◆ Permission for swimming pool or septic tank.
◆ Confirmation of the land area.
◆ Possibility of drainage, water, or electricity connections if none existing.
◆ Acceptance by *Gîtes de France* or *Clévacances* as a *chambres d'hôtes*.

They must be agreed with the vendor and if there are too many he could refuse or conclude that you are not a serious buyer and pull out altogether. If the business is to be run as a company, then the company should buy the property as it will be expensive to change afterwards. As long as this is noted, the exact name can be added later. French law is such that on death the property does not pass to a spouse, and certainly does not pass tax free, no matter what the will says. If it was bought jointly, then the spouse gets half, but only a proportion of the remainder. A *tontine* allows some of the effects of the inheritance laws to be set aside, or there is a form of company known as *Société Civile Immobilière/SCI* which is a property holding company only and is practical when several people are buying. Discuss the matter with the *notaire* because it's a complicated area and the government is loath to lose the inheritance taxes. The vendor **must** undertake termite (in some areas) and asbestos (on pre 1997 buildings) investigations, but the *notaire* usually sets these up.

You will be expected to sign the preliminary contract as soon as possible, usually within a week of your offer. You can insist on having a bilingual lawyer check the contract, and it can be signed by proxy, but it really is better if you can attend in person. The agent will be there, and if the vendor is as well then any last minute changes to the contract can be made swiftly. The *notaire* will obtain a *certificat d'urbanisme* if requested; any other conditions you must deal with yourself. The date for completion will be set (normally 60 or 90 days) but can be otherwise by agreement. Now is the time to open a French bank account as you must pay a deposit of 10–15 per cent of the purchase price.

LAND REGISTRY PLAN *(Plan Cadastral)*

All parcels of land are numbered and shown on this official plan and a copy will be attached to the deeds. If there is any doubt about a boundary, or you are not buying the whole parcel, or a *droit de passage* (right of way) has to be established, then a *géomètre* (land surveyor) has to be employed. He will set pegs in the ground to mark the boundaries and prepare a new plan if necessary. This is an excellent system as his word is law, and it avoids the squabbles over 15cm of land we suffer in the UK. The *notaire* will set up the visit and, as always, be present if you can.

FIXTURES AND FITTINGS

French owners have a tendency to go off with the fittings. Kitchen cabinets, wood burning stoves, you name it, they have all been known to disappear. Even the pendant lights have been snipped off 5cm below the ceiling. I hope they forgot to switch off the electricity before they did it! Of course you can make formal lists, but a better idea is to go and confront them and ask if they are taking anything. Have the agent along as a witness if possible and that should put a stop to it.

COMPLETION *(Acte authentique)*

If you want to cancel the sale and have not given notice 3 days before the completion date that a *clause suspensive* has not been met, then you will lose the deposit and probably have to pay the agent's fee as well. Or you could be compelled to complete. So you are probably going to go ahead. If you want a draft copy of the final sale document in advance, you will have to ask for it. You may want to take the wise precaution of having a bilingual professional check it for you. Transfer the money to France in good time. It takes several days to extract your cash from wherever it is stored and into your UK bank, for the cheque to clear, for your bank to send it to the head office of your French bank, for the cheque to clear, and for the head office to send it to your branch bank. You are expected to be present at the signing but, again, it can be done by proxy. The *notaire* keeps the deeds even when there is a mortgage, and you will receive a copy a couple of months later.

TAKING POSSESSION

The theoretical time for taking possession is midday on the day of the sale. This really means *14 heures* (2pm) as you are now a French property-owner and will need a good lunch. You will have to get used to the 24-hour clock too. You will need to contact the water, gas, electricity and telephone companies immediately to have the meters read and the accounts put into your name. If they are cut off there will be substantial re-connection charges. All property **must** have third party liability insurance.

TIPS FOR MAKING IT PAY

◆ Understand the difference between the British and French systems of conveyancing.

◆ If necessary, have conditional clauses for permissions, electricity and water services in case there are any problems.

◆ Make sure the previous owners don't take away all the fixtures and fittings.

TIP FOR IMPROVING YOUR FRENCH

◆ Listen to the BBC World Service in French

4

Renovating Your Property

THE PEOPLE YOU WILL MEET

Charpentier	Carpenter and joiner
Couvreur	Roofer
Electricien	Electrician
Entrepreneur	Builder
Maçon	Mason, bricklayer
Peintre	Painter and decorator
Plombier	Plumber

HOUSE IN GOOD CONDITION

You have decided to let a couple of spare bedrooms either in a house you already own or one bought recently with B&B in mind. There will be little or even no work required unless there aren't enough bathrooms. However, if you have just bought the house, you could easily find there are hidden problems and all is not as good as it looked on the surface. You must be warned that many French houses are not maintained to the standards we expect in the UK. One reason is the absence of building regulations as we know them in the UK. This is relevant to recent buildings and any work done to older buildings. Another reason is the absence of the surveys insisted on by building societies in the UK.

Bathrooms

Adding an en-suite bathroom to every bedroom is probably the only major alteration you **have** to do. They are a **must** these days; do not skimp on this. Try hard to incorporate them into the existing house. The cost of building an extension is unlikely ever to be recovered from running a B&B. A full bathroom is best so that you can advertise 'en-suite bathroom to all bedrooms'. However, space is at a premium and the worst thing would be to make the bedrooms uncomfortably cramped. So it may have to be a shower room, but even then always include a WC; no one accepts trotting along the corridor these days. The waste pipes from added bathrooms are always a problem, particularly the 100mm soil waste from a WC. **Do not** have a *broyeur* (electric shredder) as a means of solving this situation. They are noisy and if you have ever had to clean a blocked machine, you'll wish you had never been born.

Just possibly the former main house bathroom can be re-arranged to open off one of the bedrooms.

Services

This is the most likely area for finding problems, and with paying guests you can't afford failures. Drainage and electricity are the two most likely problematic items, and it is worthwhile having them looked at by a builder or electrician as the case may be. Also check that there is enough hot water for the extra occupants. If there is central heating, this should be checked well before the heating season; if you don't have it, perhaps this is the time to add it.

Rest of house

There is very little more that is absolutely essential, apart from making the house generally look well cared for and inviting. If the visitors' rooms are on the ground floor, could they have a separate entrance? Breakfasts will not present any problem as they can be out-of-doors, or even taken to the bedrooms, as well as at the usual dining-table. A popular option for meals is to build a conservatory (in the north of the country) or a veranda (in the south) and either of these will increase the value of the house.

OLD HOUSES NEEDING RESTORATION

Knowing Brits, it is more likely you have bought an old house that needs a lot doing to it. The French think we are quite mad and they prefer new houses for their main home, but will take on an old house in the country as a second home. Then they more or less camp there without restoring it.

You have bought an old house for its charm and character, yet have got to bring it to modern standards of comfort and sanitation. Nevertheless, work out a budget and **stick to it**. At the extreme it has been known for restoration work to cost **three times** the amount budgeted. If you spend too much, you will never make a profit on a B&B or get your money back when you sell. But the trouble with the B&B business is that standards are rising all the time. What looked adequate at the time of building may not be so ten years later. And all building work should last at least a decade. Therefore you have got to keep a sharp eye on the costs, but at the same time maintain a good standard. Also remember that when you have spent money doing up an old house, don't imagine that you now have the equivalent of a new one; the maintenance will be continuous.

Existing features

To retain the authenticity, do restore the features that give it character, not forgetting the smaller items like ironmongery and stone sinks. It is all a great expense, but afford it if you can because it is your business asset (*see Fig. 3*). Having spent the money, these antique structures need a new use. *Pigeonniers* are useful for the pool machinery, as part of a *gîte*, or how about a laundry for the guests? Bread ovens look interesting when sprayed white inside and lit, old machinery should be kept if possible. Whatever it is, be imaginative and make a feature of it.

Window with shutters

Pigeonnier

Bread oven door

Barn

Front door

Figure 3   Always preserve existing features

Replanning

You are not stuck with the same use of rooms as found existing. In
particular the dining-room and kitchen are prime candidates for moving.
The ground floors of old houses are often rather gloomy; you may find the
dining-room could be put at the back and opened up to the garden. It is not
difficult to lower the sills of windows to form a door. French kitchens are
sometimes very small. How they produce gourmet meals in them I don't
know. You need a large kitchen for a B&B with dinners.

Minimum Room Sizes:

	Bedroom for 2	Bedroom for 3	Bathroom
3 épis/clés	$14m^2$	$17m^2$	$4m^2$
4 épis/clés	$18m^2$	$17m^2$	$5m^2$

NOTIFICATION OF MINOR WORK

There is a simplified procedure for work to the exterior. It includes items such as re-roofing in a different material, creating or blocking up windows and doors, extensions of less than $20m^2$, adding a balcony or veranda, building a garage or workshop. You will be able to handle this yourself and will need to deposit the following documents at the town hall:

- Completed form.

- Location plan i.e. a portion of the local map.

- Site plan (with any extension drawn on).

- Use a photocopy of your *Plan Cadastral.*

- A sketch or photo of the state existing, and a sketch of the proposed work.

Don't worry about your artistic abilities, the merest diagram will suffice. Within a month there are three possible outcomes to the application:

- No reply is deemed to signify acceptance and the work can be started.

- Notification that it is a historic building and you must wait two months to start. You will then hear further.

- A refusal.

The acceptance lasts two years.

PRELIMINARY PLANNING PERMISSION *(Certificat d'Urbanisme)*

This is required for a new detached building or when a detached building used for anything other than habitation is to be converted to a dwelling.

A house to be used for a B&B does **not** fall into this latter category, **nor** is the certificate required for a structure physically joined onto a house such as a garage or barn. There are 2 conditions, but even if met they don't automatically guarantee permission:

1. The land must be zoned for building on the town map. If not so zoned you can always try but don't be surprised by a refusal.

2. The site must have access and be capable of connections to the services.

I trust that, if this is crucial to your business plans, you instructed the *notaire* to obtain the permission before buying the property. If not, you should be able to cope yourself as it consists of little more than filling in the form and supplying location and site plans. It is valid for 2 years and you should not assume it will automatically be renewed if it lapses.

PLANNING PERMISSION *(Permis de Construire)*

The above permissions do not allow you to build. Now you need the *Permis de Construire*. This is required for new buildings, major exterior alterations, extensions over 20 square metres and demolition. You must supply a set of drawings with plans sections and elevations, photos of the site and any existing buildings, location and site plans, details of water supply and drainage, notes of the exterior materials, and of course lengthy forms. **And** if the building is over 170m^2 in area (about the size of a 3-bedroom house) the drawings must be signed by a French-registered architect. This limit applies even for conversion of only part of the building. I recommend that you should have professional help.

However, you may reckon you have the necessary skills. Obtain the forms and comply with them scrupulously. There is, incredibly, a free service provided by the *Centre d'Architecture, d'Urbanisme et d'Environnement/ CAUE* where an architect will examine the drawings and give advice prior to submission. This may well save a refusal. As in the UK, a refusal is hard to reverse.

Do not start work without the permission. It only lasts for 2 years, and if it is about to run out start the work in some small way. Consult with the town hall for a historically listed building.

BUILDING REGULATIONS

For carrying out the work you, or your builder, must:

- Display the required board.
- Notify when work has started.
- Notify when work has finished.

Basically therefore general building regulations don't exist, it's up to the individual builder to take out insurance to guarantee that the work is sound. Obviously there are strict regulations for all the services, but they are administered by the companies concerned.

USING AN ARCHITECT

When to use an architect

If the restoration work is minor you will make your own decisions. When it involves major structural work, substantial re-planning of the inside, and certainly if you are practically gutting the place, then please do use an architect. Why do all that work and yet not make the very best use of the building? Obviously I would say that since I am one myself. Well here is a small example of the kind of benefit. I complimented a proprietor on the way he had converted a double bedroom into a family room by adding a mezzanine going up into the roof space. He said, 'The architect thought of that.' Honest, he didn't know I'm one myself.

The architect's work

This is to obtain all necessary permissions and, if engaged, take the project to completion; in which case he will find and conduct all negotiations with builders. One of his tasks is to keep the project within budget. In inexperienced hands the cost can mount to alarming heights and an architect's fee will have been more than spent. Visit 2 or 3 firms and discuss fees – they should preferably be located near the project. Usually the first visit is free; if a scheme is aborted there will be a charge. You will be expected to sign a contract. If you are doing the building work yourself an architect can be employed to do the drawings and get the permission but it is not necessary always to have the full service.

LARGE BUILDING PROJECTS

Choosing a builder

By employing a local builder to do some immediate work, which included a new bathroom and septic tank, we managed to welcome the first paying guest three months after we arrived, and the business was up and running. We employed mostly French workmen and found them competent and hard-working. Nothing ever got finished on time – so what's new? We also used some English builders and one Australian. The advantage there is that you can take up references as their clients will also be mainly ex-pats.

The criteria for choosing builders is **not** the same as for private work. They must be prompt, must clean up, and must finish everything completely. These attributes are more important than saving the last sou. Finding builders when you first arrive is difficult. Ask your neighbours, or ask the estate agent who sold you the house. If you take a name from the *Yellow Pages*, ask for their *SIRET* number. If they have one they are properly registered at the *Chambre de Commerce*.

The personnel

The normal method of building is to employ each trade separately. This poses problems if you do not speak French and have absolutely no experience of building, or will be absent much of the time. If any of these apply, it is better to employ an *enterprise générale de bâtiment* (general contractor), though it will cost a little more.

The trades are:

Carpenter and joiner	Mason
Decorator	Plumber
Electrician	Roofer

For all building work you must realise that if you go home, they will. There are goats to tend, chickens to feed, and all manner of other urgent jobs. So, if possible, you should stay around or try to visit at least once a fortnight, or have someone else do so and report on progress. Builders will start at 8am and take a 2-hour lunch break at 12.00. Like everyone else, they are bound to the 35-hour week unless self employed. Do not proffer mugs of tea or coffee; it is not the custom. Sunday is the day for the family, therefore business calls are not welcome.

Paying

Never pay the whole sum in advance, but you will probably be asked for a deposit of 15 per cent and some money as the work progresses if it is extensive. For a private householder the *TVA* is 5.5 per cent for renovation and 19.6 per cent for new building. For a *TVA*-registered business, all building is at 19.6 per cent which will be refunded in due course. It is expected that you will raise queries on the final bill, but you must get a reputation as a **prompt payer**, or no one will work for you.

Insurance

When the work is finished, it will be guaranteed for 1 year. After that the builder **must** have insurance to cover the work for defects. It runs for 10 years for structural work, 2 years for other work, and 1 year for alterations. If you have set up a substantial amount of work without professional help, you are advised to have insurance yourself to cover an expert handling any claims on your behalf.

MINOR BUILDING PROJECTS

Assuming the amount of building work is not large and you are not doing it all yourself, then you will be engaging the various tradesmen. Your biggest problem will be keeping to a budget. The causes of increased costs are:

- Not giving complete and clear instructions.
- Not getting firm quotations.
- Last minute changes.
- Delays of your own making.
- Unforeseen problems.

The latter can only be solved by keeping some money back for contingencies. The remainder are entirely your own fault.

Instructions

If a builder doesn't know precisely what you want, he can't prepare an accurate quotation. If you are without professional help, prepare a 'shopping list' of what is required. List it room by room, very simply, i.e. 'new window'. At the end, list all the items you are going to buy yourself. If it needs to be in French, I'm sure errors of grammar will be forgiven.

Quotations *(Devis)*

If you can, ask two or three people to quote (if you can find that many). If no reply arrives within a fortnight, chase it; it looks businesslike. The builder should submit 2 copies of the quotation. He will have signed the original; you then sign and return it, and it becomes the contract. The snag with this system is the quotation is often only 6 sentences long, when it would take several closely printed pages to specify the work properly. All you can do is question him closely on the extent of the work and what is included. If major items seem to be missing, don't be afraid to ask him to re-submit the quotation. It should have stated the time for the work; it won't be kept to but is a help when progress is slow. We found tradesmen generally willing to return and attend to any small problems after the work is completed.

Changes

Make up your mind. Changes made after receipt of the quotation leave you wide open to substantial extra costs. Even small alterations have repercussions you never realised.

Delays

It is quite normal for you to buy some items direct such as sanitary fittings, wood burning stove, wall tiles. But you must order them in time. If a builder has to wait, it will cost extra. Check if delivery is included because quite often it isn't. Some shops have vans for hire or take it in your own vehicle if possible. We came home one day with a bath on the roof rack; we simply didn't want to miss a special offer!

BUILDING-IT-YOURSELF

Competence

Do not take on too much. You have come to France to run a B&B, not to learn the building trade. One thing is certain: it will take longer. I have known it take three years before the first paying guest arrived. Of course it is cheaper, but you have lost all that period of income. Try and phase the work by finishing a couple of bedrooms and the dining-room first. Then do later phases by closing for the winter when there's hardly anyone about anyway and work can proceed unhindered. In southern France even outside work can continue through the winter. Building is dangerous work – did you see the programme on TV a while back about the chap who cut off his own hand (they sewed it back on)? Do take care. Amateurs always find it hard to work to a deadline, but the cement mixer and materials must be cleared away by the end of April.

Assistance

You will need to employ tradesmen for some of the work. A French electrician is **essential**, probably also roofer, plasterer, and plumber. Do not bring over your British mates; it does not go down well. The thrifty Dutch have the reputation of bringing all their workmen and materials. The caustic comment is 'they even bring their own sandwiches'.

Materials

Paint is cheaper in Britain, but otherwise do not bring your own materials. The French, too, are very keen on *bricolage* (DIY) and there are plenty of well-stocked shops; some are vast emporiums. There are also sanitary fitting suppliers with vast stocks, general builders' merchants, timber yards, and specialist joinery shops. Unfortunately, as a newcomer and a foreigner, you may not at first get the discounts a builder would normally expect. If you establish a good relationship with a smaller supplier, they will give much more helpful advice than the big chains.

Building practice

To suit differing climates, every country constructs their houses accordingly and you will have to find out French methods. One way is to snoop in on any building sites nearby. France still has excellent stonemasons and joiners with very high standards of craftsmanship. But bricklaying is not their forte.

THE BUILDING WORK

Get the priorities right. This is a true story: the previous owners had put in a new bathroom with a pink suite including his'n'hers washbasins. Very posh if you like pink. But the drain went to a ditch.

Structural work inside and out	Drainage
Re-building chimneys	Timber treatment
Re-roofing and new gutters	New stairs
Plan for new bathrooms even if not to be built yet	Sandblasting inside

Figure 4 This work MUST be done first

Some work can be done later, but remember that all building work makes a mess.

New doors and windows	Plastering and floor finishes
New partitions	Central heating and insulation
Pointing stone and brickwork	Fitting out bathrooms and kitchens
Extensions	

Figure 5 This work can be done later

Roof

Tiled roofs originally had oak boarding and hand-made tiles which are very heavy. It is a kindness to old timbers to lighten the load with modern interlocking tiles but they do not look authentic. If possible, use clay tiles made to the traditional shapes. Thatch should be replaced with matching materials. Chimneys are often in a bad state and need complete re-building. Country houses originally did not have gutters but they have usually been added, town houses now all have gutters. Look in heavy rain for leaks.

Exterior walls

For new walls, the ideal is to match the original stone or brick. Nowadays they have an inside skin of *brique* (insulated clay bricks); cavity walls are not used. If you really cannot afford this, then it will have to be the modern standard of *brique* with rendering outside. Some very old brick walls are built of sun-dried bricks, and, because these are so weak, they usually have the corners and openings reinforced with fired bricks. These soft bricks cannot be left without rendering. For repairs to exposed brickwork, always use reclaimed bricks. Old stone and brick walls may need re-pointing. Be careful here, as if amateurishly done, it can spoil the look of the whole building. Damp-proof courses are a late nineteenth-century invention and I do not know of any satisfactory way of inserting them in stone or timber frame walls; brick walls can be dealt with by specialists.

For damp walls, the water has to be stopped either with a land drain outside or waterproofing inside, or both. The trouble with farm houses is that originally the ground floor was for the animals, and the humans lived on the first floor all nice and dry. So for any part of the house which is below ground and for damp basements, you will have to call on specialists. New openings should have lintels to match those existing and windows should have a vertical proportion, not the modern horizontal. A good mason will make new openings and move existing ones in brickwork or stone so that you will hardly know the work has been done – at a cost of course.

Floors

Really old houses had beaten earth on the lowest floor, but probably something has been done by now, even if only paving on top of the earth. A new concrete slab gives the opportunity to include a damp-proof membrane and insulation. On upper floors old oak beams with 2cm thick boards are the epitome of character. Not much of this boarding has survived to the present century. It is possible to replace bad areas with second-hand boards, but you will have to accept uneven floors and propping under the furniture legs to make them stand evenly. The problem with replacing oak boards with modern thin pine is that the beams are too far apart. Either you have to accept a bouncy floor or move the beams closer together.

Sound insulation of wood floors is difficult and is a particular problem if one bedroom is above another. Thick carpets are one solution, or have the new laminated planks, but they must be laid on a 7mm insulating underlay. Buy good quality and have it properly laid.

A bathroom above a bedroom is an even worse problem. A solution is to raise it a step. The space is filled with insulation and it has the added benefit of making the pipe runs easier. But the WC flushing in the small hours will still be heard. If the whole structure of the floor has to be replaced, consider the system of pre-cast concrete T-shaped beams with blocks laid in between and screed on top. This is ultra-modern construction but gives excellent sound insulation between floors and total freedom of choice of finish on top.

Timber pests

Woodworm and beetle are rife in France. Treat the timbers before any other work, and again later, and again. But the pests are only kept at bay, not eliminated. Termites have appeared in some areas but the previous owners will have had a compulsory inspection in the three months before the sale of the property. If you suspect dry rot, call in the experts.

Doors, windows, shutters

There may be original doors; if so, keep them. Otherwise, please do not have flush doors; they look so cheap and out of character. Doors come complete with frames, hinges, lock, and glazing where required. Windows are unlikely to be original, so it is a matter of their condition and your pocket if you replace them. Windows also come complete with ironmongery and glazing. Only have double glazing if you are having new windows anyway; it does not pay to change. Choose windows with glazing bars to match the original ones; big panes look very modern. All windows open inwards so that you can reach the shutters, and the French will expect working shutters to the bedrooms. They have the double purpose of keeping the sun out (in which case they should be latched slightly open) or as double glazing (when they should be fully shut). If any of this joinery has to be purpose-made to special sizes, which is very likely, there are excellent joinery works. Window frames should be of wood, not plastic or metal.

Stairs

Old stairs will either be grandiose or miserably steep and narrow. If a new flight is necessary, don't have winders (tapered treads) as shown in the glossy joinery brochures and which are common in French houses. They are dangerous for children and not suitable for adults carrying luggage. If the stair needs to change direction, have a ¼ or ½ landing. Have a firm handrail for the whole flight, and no opening in the balustrade should be more than 11cm (so that children can't get their heads through).

Inside walls

If load bearing, they will be *brique* again. Do not replace load bearing walls with a beam without professional help. Partitions these days are of metal stud and plasterboard. If between bedrooms or bedroom and bathroom, then the space between the studs should be filled with glass wool for sound insulation. This gives some improvement, but good sound insulation is impossible to achieve in old buildings. Old plaster may need replacing because it is loose or soft. The walls can be lined with plaster board, but this gives a very modern feel. In really old houses it's better to re-render, following the less-than-straight contours of the existing wall. Stone walls internally can be sand-blasted. This looks superb but is laborious because it will need re-pointing afterwards. Possibly do this on the ground floor only.

Heating

If you intend to stay open in the winter, then you **must** have central heating even in the south. The winters are certainly shorter there but are still cold. Oil is the cheapest fuel at the moment, but real chefs prefer to cook with gas so this may influence the choice. Underfloor heating has come back into favour, but it has a slow warm-up period which is a disadvantage to a B&B, so stay with radiators.

Open fires are for ambience, not serious heating. Wood-burning stoves are more economical but a lot of work and do not heat the whole house. If you have not got central heating, it will have to be electricity; check out oil-filled radiators and storage heaters; they are improving all the time. The fuse board can be set up so that the electric heaters cut out first if the system is overloaded. An overload is very likely on a cold morning in a B&B when everyone is getting up and everything is on all at once. Insulate the loft space of course. A word of warning on insulation: mice find polystyrene very cosy too and we cursed the day we ever allowed the stuff in the house.

Heating large double-height spaces such as a converted barn is difficult because there is just not enough wall space for the number of radiators required. The best method is a warm air system such as is found in small village halls. You would find heating a big space like this just for a couple of breakfasts to be totally uneconomic.

Solar energy has not yet become commonplace in France, but you could consider it as you need a lot of heating and hot water. There is even a government grant until 2006, so ask a specialist installer for details. But do site the panels discreetly if on an old roof.

Water

The water supply has been privatised and there are several companies. In some areas it is very hard. All water is metered. There never were water tanks in the roof space so you won't find them even in older houses. Healthwise it is drinkable from the tap; tastewise it is a matter of preference.

You need **plenty** of hot water. The peak time is just before dinner. People have just arrived, or are changing for dinner, or putting tots to bed. Everyone in fact is bathing or showering all at once, so a big well-insulated cylinder is essential. If run from the central heating boiler, it will cost ⅔ less than electricity. The very well-insulated cylinders are usually situated in the roof space; airing cupboards are unknown. If space is really difficult to find for a normal cylinder, there are pressurized types, but they are a job for an expert only. Be scrupulous about insulating pipes because a freeze-up will bring the business to a standstill.

Electricity

The monopoly is still part government owned, though that is likely to change. The company is *Electricité de France/EDF*. The voltage is 220/230 the same as the UK, but the wiring system is entirely different. **Do not** have a British electrician install a ring main circuit. The electricity company will refuse to connect, and it is extremely dangerous to a French electrician working on the installation in the future. A disadvantage of the system is that the location of heavy-duty appliances such as dishwashers, washing machines and heaters have to be specified in advance. But an advantage of the system is that shavers and hair dryers can be run from the light fitting over the basin without further provision. Internal bathrooms and WCs need mechanical ventilation and it can be noisy. Electricity is cheaper than in many other countries because of the huge amount generated by atomic power stations, and because most of the power lines are overhead. This latter makes for more cuts to the supply than we are used to.

Gas

The company is *Gaz de France/GDF* and is a joint company, *EDF/GDF*, with the electricity company. Mains gas is available in towns only. Elsewhere you can have a large cylinder placed outdoors or even underground – only worth it for central heating. Or you can have two cylinders outside near the point of use and with an automatic changeover. **Do not** have the small cylinders positioned under the worktop as they need changing manually. You have to remember to keep a spare and they run out at the most inconvenient times. **Do not** have a local gas water heater where there is a shower, because they require different water pressures.

Drainage

In conurbations you will be connected to main drainage just as in Britain. Don't worry if it has to be pumped uphill; it's a not uncommon necessity. In the country you will have a septic tank. Don't worry about it; they are really no trouble. For a B&B it's most unlikely that an existing installation will be large enough. For a new one the rules are much stricter than they used to be because of fears of pollution. You will need an *étude* (study) to assess the impact of the proposed tank, then you will need permission. It is best left in the hands of a specialist builder who will get the permission and do the work. The main thing is to build a large enough one to cope with any future expansion.

Children's safety

All glass in windows and doors below 90cm height should be safety glass or have protective film applied (this film is available in DIY stores). Any upstairs window sills below 90cm height should have a balustrade outside to prevent children climbing out; these are usually wrought iron and actually look very decorative.

Disabled provision

The bedroom and its en-suite shower room **must** be on the ground floor. You should ask *Gîtes de France* or *Clévacances* for guidance and the detailed requirements.

ardoise (f)	slate	isolation (f)	insulation
amiante (m)	asbestos	linteau (m)	lintel
béton (m)	concrete	livraison (f)	delivery
béton armé	reinforced concrete	mansarde (f)	loft
bois exotique (m)	hardwood	marche (f)	step
bricolage (m)	do-it-yourself	mazout (f)	heating oil
brique (m)	brick	menuiserie (f)	joinery
carreau (m)	wall/floor tile	peinture (f)	paint
carrelage (m)	tiling	peinture acrylique	emulsion paint
chaudière (f)	boiler	persienne (f)	louvred shutter
chauffage (m)	heating	pierre (f)	stone
chauffage central	central heating	pin (m)	pine
chaume (m)	thatch	plafond (m)	ceiling
cheminée (f)	chimney	plancher (m)	floor
couche (f)	coat (of paint)	plâtre (m)	plaster
crépi (m)	textured coating	porte (f)	door
devis (m)	estimate	porte fenêtre	French window
électricité (m)	electricity	porte d'entrée	front door
électrique	electric	pouter (f)	beam
escalier (m)	stairs	prise (f)	electric socket
escabeau (m)	step-ladder	quinquaillerie (f)	ironmongery
(à l')étage	on the first floor	radiateur (m)	radiator
fenêtre (f)	window	rez-de-chaussée (m)	ground floor
fiche (f)	electric plug	robinet d'arrêt (m)	stopcock
fil (m)	wire	traveaux (f)	building work
fosse (m)	ditch	tuile (f)	roof tile
fosse septique	septic tank	tuyau (m)	pipe
four à pain (m)	bread oven	vitre (f)	pane of glass
gaz (m)	gas	vitrage (f)	glazing
gouttière (f)	gutter	double vitrage	double glazing
interrupteur (m)	switch	volet (m)	shutter

Figure 6   Glossary

TIPS FOR MAKING IT PAY

◆ Employ an architect to get the best out of your building.

◆ Get firm quotations from builders.

◆ Do not take on too much DIY.

TIP FOR IMPROVING YOUR FRENCH

◆ Read a French newspaper such as *Le Monde* or *Le Figaro*.

5

Planning the Inside of Your B&B

AMBIENCE

Why stay in a B&B? What else is there? There are:

Chain hotels – blandly uniform, see one and you've seen them all; totally impersonal

Small family run hotels – quality varies, some absolutely delightful, some dreadful

Large hotels – at the cheaper end impersonal, at the luxury level superb

Therefore, to be an attractive alternative to the competition, a B&B has to have a welcoming, friendly, individual atmosphere, but yet not be **so** homely that paying guests feel embarrassed to be intruding in someone else's private life. It's quite difficult to get the right balance between formality and informality, so my advice is to err on the side of formality. Keep the rooms free of too much personal clutter. Obviously most of the furniture will be pieces you already have, but you will find that much of it isn't suitable, and you should be ruthless about discarding any that looks tired and can't be freshened up. New furniture should be stout and serviceable, but avoid plastic, metal and chipboard as much as possible and keep to wood for a warmer feeling. It has to be admitted that a few B&Bs let the side down badly, and French hotel wallpaper has a world reputation for awfulness. The possible faults are so numerous I'll leave them to your imagination.

buanderie (f)	utility room	salle de bain (f)	bathroom
cave (f)	cellar	salle de jeux (f)	games room
chambre (f)	bedroom	salle à manger (f)	dining room
couloir (m)	corridor	salon (m)	lounge
cuisine (f)	kitchen	sous-sol (m)	basement
grenier (m)	attic	toilettes (f)	lavatory
placard (m)	cupboard	veranda (f)	veranda
salle d'eau (f)	shower room	vestibule (m)	hall

Figure 7   The rooms

I regret I'm not that keen on the cheaper end of French furniture, especially what they call *ambiance d'autrefois* (period furniture). I find it dark, heavy and very pseudo. Though their best is as good as anyone's, that is not for a B&B. I'll fly the flag and say that moderately priced furniture is better designed in Britain. However you can't anticipate everything you'll need and will have to shop in France sooner or later. There's a branch of Ikea in all the big towns but as it's all flat pack you have to make it up. For the *4-épis* château you could go and look in a branch of Roche Bobois for furnishing ideas for a period property, even if you don't buy there. Antiques are **very** expensive in France. If you want a few period pieces go to furniture auctions in the UK before you move, but beware that neither the guests, their children, nor the cleaning lady will be as careful with them as you would wish.

Avoid clutter but give the establishment some character by displaying your personal interests; they make a good talking point. Put on show any previous sporting trophies or photos, or items from hobbies or jobs. Enlarge a photo of your great grandparents and put it in a heavy fame. Confine the pictures to those you appreciate yourself, then make a really positive statement by having them large or perhaps five or six in a row – something that will dominate the room.

Some practical points:

- Fix **everything** securely: mirrors, pictures, handrails.

- **Do not** have too many notices or you'll look like a dragon of a seaside landlady.

- Breakable items such as vases, lamps, ornaments **will get broken**, so don't put out the family heirlooms

BEDROOMS

Beds

For one room, you'd better have twin beds. For 2, 3, or 4 rooms, have one room with twin beds and the rest double. For 5 or 6 rooms have two twin and the rest double. If the room is large enough, then one double and one single is a good combination and is called a family room, but it can also be let as either a double or a twin room. We had two family rooms, in fact one was large enough to take a folding bed as well, and during the summer holiday, they were filled from end to end with a family, but the rest of the year they were just double bedrooms. Single rooms are not worth it unless you have a room so small that it will only take a single bed, because they need a shower room the same size as a double room.

Although most British and French couples opt for a double bed, some nationalities such as American, German, Scandinavian and Japanese prefer twin beds. The Dutch like large beds, single or double, since they are tall people.

French beds are the same standard sizes as British ones:

Single	90 × 190cm
Double	140 × 190cm
Queen	150 × 200cm
King	160 × 200cm

If you have a small room adjoining the main bedroom or a mezzanine, which is designated only for children, then you could have 80cm-wide single beds or bunks, otherwise these are considered sub-standard. A width of 80cm is acceptable for a folding bed as that is also only for children. You will need a cot, though it won't often be used as most people bring their own.

Good quality beds and mattresses (sprung please) are **essential**, so how come some proprietors miss out? Bed heads are necessary, but anything at the foot only slows the bed making.

For the grade 4 level you should consider the larger bed sizes and the possibility of a four poster or one of the many varieties of canopy. The room should be limited to two people; it is expected that children will have a separate room.

Other furnishing

The contents of hotel rooms are very carefully considered, and B&B owners can learn a lot from them. Before the guests arrive, the room should look just a touch on the empty side because you'll be amazed at what clients bring in these people carriers. Wardrobes are best built in; freestanding ones collect cobwebs behind and are a bother if the floor isn't 100% level. They don't need to be large. A single door width provides enough hanging space, but shelves for clothes in the same cupboard are better than a chest of drawers as they can be checked at a glance for things left behind. Have a table rather than a dressing-table, then it does for writing as well, with a stool or chair. Guests spend a lot of time in the bedroom so it needs to be comfortable. If there's room, have a couple of small arm chairs; they can be wicker, otherwise it'll have to be a couple of ordinary chairs. If you do have a chest of drawers, it needs a piece of 5mm glass with polished edges for the top, as both alcohol and beauty products leave stains. Guests do need somewhere to put cases, so either provide extra space in the wardrobe or a stand. The latter suits one-night people better as they don't unpack, not that some longer stay people do either. Whether you provide somewhere for cases or not, they will be stored on the floor, under the bed, or on top of the wardrobe. For bedside tables, the round chipboard ones will seem the cheapest, but by the time you've bought sets of circular cloths, plus either a washable one for the top or had a piece of glass cut, you could have bought a wood cabinet.

To complete the ensemble: bedside tables, pictures and bedside mats if the room isn't carpeted. A full length mirror is appreciated especially by those going to a wedding.

armoire (f)	cupboard	lits superposés	bunk beds
cadre (m)	picture frame	literie (f)	bedding
chaise (f)	chair	matelas (m)	mattress
chevet (m)	bedside table	matelas en mousse	foam mattress
commode (m)	chest of drawers	matelas à ressorts	sprung mattress
descente de lit (f)	bedside mat	miroir (m)	mirror
dosseret (m)	bedhead	moquette (f)	fitted carpet
fauteuil (m)	arm chair	penderie (f)	wardrobe
lit (m)	bed	placard (m)	built in cupboard
lit à baldaquin	four poster	table (f)	table
lit de bébé	cot	table de toilette	dressing table
lit double	double bed	tablette (f)	shelf
lits jumeaux	twin beds	tableau (f)	picture
lit pliant	folding bed	tapis (m)	mat, rug
lit simple	single bed		

Figure 8   Bedroom furniture

Finishes

You'll have noticed that most hotels have carpet on the floor; it really is the quietest. And it is the easiest to keep clean provided it is a neutral colour with a slight texture. No need to buy the best quality. Boarding, whether old or new, always looks good but is noisy. The modern laminated wood flooring looks alright, though it doesn't fool anyone that it's genuine solid wood. But if poorly laid without enough expansion all round, it does not lie flat. Expansion is especially necessary at all doors. The cheaper quality is very susceptible to damp, and in the bedrooms damp can come from leaking radiators, overflowing en-suite bathrooms, windows left open, leaking roofs, frozen pipes, to name but a few. Tiles are suitable for the south and they can be laid on boarding with an underlay. For the walls it's paint or paper. If paint, there's the emulsion we know so well, there's a textured paint called *crépi*, or there's an expensive range called *Murs d'Autrefois* specially for the antique look. If you decide to paper, please go easy on the pattern. 'French hotel wallpaper' is a derogatory term. For the ceiling I wouldn't have anything other than white or the room looks gloomy.

Heating

The problem with heating guest bedrooms is they need to be to a living-room level of 19°C rather than a household bedroom level of 16°C. This is so that the room feels warm to walk into and because guests use it like a living-room to sit in. Which means it has to be heated for all those hours when they are out. When there aren't any guests booked, you could keep the heating on low and provide an electric fan heater if anyone turns up, though it's not ideal. You will obviously think hard about how many rooms to keep open in the winter.

Electricity

For general lighting, obviously you need a central pendant or wall brackets. For bedside lights, a pair of wall brackets is much better than bedside lamps as the latter do get broken. Guests also need a socket handy for recharging all their gadgets at your expense. The vacuum cleaner needs one anyway.

Themes

Some owners theme their rooms. I've heard of them being named after artists (French of course) with reproductions in the room, and that sounds interesting. I've seen others named after flowers or colours and that just seems naff. So, unless done with flair, don't. We numbered our rooms, which some *Gîtes de France* don't like as being too much like a hotel.

Finishing touches

It will not be expected that a B&B will have a room telephone and I'd be cautious about a TV because of sound transmission. If you have a mainly British clientele they will appreciate (or even expect) a tea-making facility, but it's not very common in France so it's not essential. Lastly, the room needs **4** door keys, one for the guests, one for the cleaner, one for when the guest goes home with theirs and does not post it back, and one for emergencies.

Now sleep in **each** of the bedrooms yourself for a week.

BATHROOMS

'Is there enough hot water?', asks Mrs Brit-with-the-cut-glass-accent on being shown her en-suite bathroom. Basil Fawlty would have had an answer to that, something like, 'Put another log on, Manuel. The lady needs a bath.'

The bathroom is so important now that I wonder if we shouldn't advertise 'bathroom with en-suite bedroom'. An en-suite bath or shower room is **essential** these days. 'H&C in all rooms' (euphemism for a washbasin) with the WC down the corridor just won't do any more. There's nothing for it but to provide a separate facility for each room, whatever it costs, which is a lot; and no cheating like putting a pre-fabricated shower cubicle in the corner. Whether to have bath or shower rooms depends on the standard of your establishment and the available space. At grade 4 it needs to be bathrooms; at grade 3 it can be either.

The insertion of a bathroom into existing rooms needs careful planning, and I've seen examples where it's been badly done, in a situation where it could have been so much better. It's best to try and get as near the hotel standard plan as possible, see *Fig. 9*. If this can't be done then try and make it as unobtrusive as possible, see *Fig. 10*. A large square room needs an imaginative solution; see *Fig. 11* for an interesting idea.

The trouble with a mix at different prices is that it makes for complications in the bookings. We got it wrong once and gave a shower room to someone who had been promised a bathroom. There was a hell of a fuss. I'm stating the obvious when I say that baths take a lot of hot water. It wouldn't be so bad if everyone didn't bathe at the same time, which is just before dinner. They've got the time and you are providing free hot water, aren't you? Save on the sanitary ware and have all white, but spend on the taps because they get hard use. Ease of cleaning is paramount and everything should be considered from that standpoint; there should be the minimum of exposed pipework.

Bath

Have a normal 170cm-long bath with a shower fitting. Don't go for oddities like a small size bath, an extra long one, or a jacuzzi. The latter are noisy

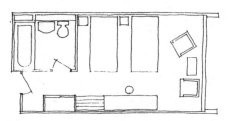

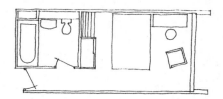

A STANDARD HOTEL BEDROOMS

Figure 9 Adding bathrooms

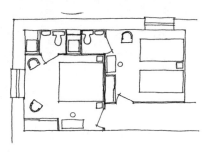

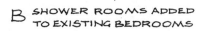

B SHOWER ROOMS ADDED TO EXISTING BEDROOMS

Figure 10

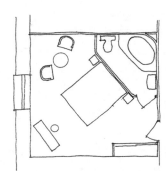

C BATHROOM ADDED TO LARGE EXISTING BEDROOM

Figure 11

and need explaining how to use. The best-looking screen to the bath/shower is the single leaf glass frameless type. At grade 4 you will have to spend a lot on the bathroom, and, if there's room, a free-standing bath looks very trendy. In any case, the shower should be a separate fitting.

Basin

A basin set into a vanity top is much the easiest to keep clean, but don't have a cabinet below. In fact don't have any cupboards in the bathroom: too difficult to keep clean. Even a pedestal is a nuisance, have the basin

abattant (m)	WC seat	mélangeur (m)	mixer tap
beignoire (f)	bath tub	plan de toilette (m)	vanity top
cabine de douche (f)	shower cubicle	porte-serviettes (m)	towel rail
douche (f)	shower	receveur (m)	shower tray
lavabo (f)	basin	robinet (m)	tap
lave-mains (m)	hand-wash basin	WC (m)	WC

Figure 12 Bathroom fittings

on brackets if no vanity top. At grade 4 you should try and have two basins.

WC

If possible, have the suspended type with a concealed cistern, all in the interests of easy cleaning. Most are dual flush these days and you can get a silencing mechanism for most models (they're not all that silent). The French are still wary of the WC opening directly off the bedroom, or being situated in the bathroom, but the since the rest of the world accepts it, just keep the room smelling nice with a proprietary product. With a septic tank, some owners put notices up about restrictions. We didn't and were lucky enough never to have any trouble.

Bidet

I know France is the home of this article, but don't bother. The bum-washing function has now been taken over by the shower.

Shower

No one likes the smallest tray size of 75 × 75cm, so do have something larger. But, whatever you do, there's likely to be trouble when it's sited on a wooden floor. **Serious trouble**. Shower cubicles leak and do real damage to the house. The problem is likely to be hidden for a long time, until one day a portion of the floor or ceiling collapses. We tried curtains, folding doors, sliding doors, notices in several languages and still we had trouble from 3 out of 5 of our showers upstairs. The worst offenders are unsupervised children. 'Oh I'm terribly sorry,' said a mother when we hammered on the door because water was pouring through the kitchen ceiling onto that night's dinner. She was sitting reading while her six-year-old showered without shutting the screen door. Some adults are not all that careful either. There's really no foolproof system for upstairs showers, but the best screens are glass in a metal frame. Plastic panels and frame can warp which means the doors don't close tightly. A downstairs shower with a tiled concrete floor can stand some water so you could have a walk-in cubicle with a fixed screen and no moving parts. There should be a thermostatic mixing valve, and since the flexible hoses have a very short life when used carelessly, you could consider building the fitting in.

Tiling

For the floor, have light-coloured tiles with dark joints. Light tiles don't show the dirt, and conversely dark joints don't show the dirt. I know you're going to be clean but no one's perfect. Laying the tiles diagonally looks good and conceals the fact of any walls not being at right angles. The cost of wall tiles varies enormously. Ignoring the institutional white, I would go for something moderately priced and then tile the whole room. Add a contrasting tiled dado line just above the basin and the room will look very smart. A final touch is to have the tiles above the dado a slightly lighter colour than the ones below.

Sundries

You need a towel rail or rack, mirror, glass shelf, waste bin, toilet-roll holder, soap dishes, somewhere for the spare toilet rolls, WC brush, tooth mug, something to hang the handwashed smalls on: in fact almost a trolley-full of items per bathroom from the DIY store. Note: a bin is **essential** or you could get nappies down the drain, with disastrous results. The bathroom lock should be of the type that is openable from the outside, as the last thing you need is a child locked in, though I realise that specialist ironmongery of this kind is only obtainable from builders' merchants. A window needs a roller blind or curtain or both.

People do need enough space to put all the toiletries/medecines/sponge bags they bring these days, so provide either enough shelf space or a decent vanity top. One dear soul arrived with 20 beauty products (yes, I did count, I couldn't resist it).

The elderly need some safety measures in the bathroom. Provide a stool and hand grips to the bath and shower. Could you also place a rubber safety mat somewhere discreet?

KITCHEN

Breakfasts

An ordinary domestic kitchen is fine for breakfasts only. Or you could set up a mini kitchen in the actual dining room or a conservatory, and trolley the dirties to the dishwasher in the house kitchen. If you have an old house with a kitchen straight out of *Country Living* magazine, and only a couple of guest bedrooms, you could serve breakfasts there. You'd have to be super-tidy, unable to use it as a kitchen until they've finished eating and chatting, and accept that guests will invade it at any time of day because they will not regard it as private.

Dinners

This is a different matter. A lot will depend on the policy of your local inspector. If you do a lot of dinners they might be quite rigorous while in other areas they make no demands at all. In any case, a domestic kitchen is not really suitable, yet the scale of operations does not justify the big expense of a commercial installation. So the only thing to do is to get as near the commercial standard as possible. The room should be twice the area found in most modern houses, with a big central table.

A commercial kitchen has:
   – White wall tiles throughout
   – High level of fluorescent lighting
   – Glazed tile floor
   – All fittings and double sink/double drainer in stainless steel
   – Large gas cooker with extract hood
   – Open shelves for utensils and china
   – Walk-in larder for dry goods
   – Flat plastered ceiling
   – All fittings raised above floor level on legs to discourage vermin
   – Dishwasher

It would also have a walk-in cold store, but you'll have a big domestic larder-fridge and a chest freezer. The normal 12-place 60cm-wide dishwasher will probably have to do, though actually they only just about cope with 10 people and that's providing you don't put the pots and pans in. There are domestic machines available for 16 place settings at twice the price and they are 80cm wide. All commercial machines and cookers are very expensive. If you need a gas supply for the kitchen only, have the large double cylinders which are located outside. Worktops should be plastic, not tiled.

congélateur (m)	freezer	lave linge (m)	washing machine
évier (m)	sink	lave vaisselle (m)	dishwasher
frigo (m)	fridge	micro-onde (f)	microwave
four (m)	oven	plan de travail (m)	worktop
grille-pain (m)	toaster	plaque de cuisson (f)	hob top
hotte (f)	cooker hood	réfrigérateur (m)	refrigerator

Figure 13 Kitchen fittings

Crockery, glassware, cutlery

Things get lost or broken at a fast rate, mostly by yourselves because you're pushed for time. Therefore **do not** use your own good quality stuff. Hotel quality china is available from 'cash and carries' and really is less breakable; plus you'll be able to get matching replacements easily. I'm sure you will have it all matching anyway. Don't have the crockery that is actually made of glass; it's considered cheap. The quantity of everything needs to be **at least** 1 ½ times the number of people, i.e. 12 of everything for 8 people. This allows for breakages or items found to be dirty at the last minute. It happens. Wine glasses must be treated as a totally expendable stock; buy 19cl goblets, nothing fancy. Steak knives are commonly used, but fish knives and forks are not essential.

Safety

We had a fire extinguisher and fire blanket, even though these were not mandatory. Unfortunately a smoke detector sounds off at the first hint of burning toast, so it would have to be a heat detector if anything at all.

DINING ROOM

Setting the scene

To the French, the conviviality of the table is one of the essential ingredients of the menu. Therefore, as part of the family atmosphere, *chambres d'hôtes* are expected to have one large table. This doesn't always suit the insular British, so it had better be mentioned in your brochure. Only once did we have two couples sit in stony silence throughout the meal. Usually it was the reverse with continuous chatter, sometimes in three languages, and showing a great unwillingness to leave the table. You just have to clear the crocks and leave them to it. It is not the French custom to have the coffee elsewhere, so don't try and move them unless it's an all British group. Even after breakfast people often wanted to chatter on, but then we did shoo them away at ten o'clock. If the dining-room is a separate room you are lucky because it can laid or cleared at your leisure.

Furnishing

Finding a large enough table can be difficult and for more than 8 it is extremely heavy (*see Fig. 14*). How about buying two and putting them together? This means they can be separated when there are only two people. The table must be big enough for **all** the guests at once. Even for breakfasts, they could all come down at once, especially if they are a group. Chairs should not be too heavy because the floor needs sweeping after every meal. There needs to be a sideboard for possibly putting some of the breakfast things on and for dishes and plates when serving dinner. Any other furnishings are for creating the right atmosphere.

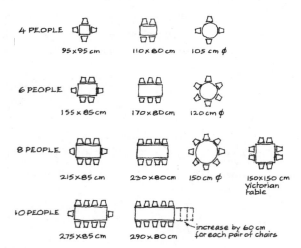

Figure 14 Dining table sizes

Finishes

The French are untidy eaters – to our prim British eyes anyway – and the floor will be full of crumbs; it's even worse when there are babies. So **do not** have carpet. Tiles are much the best, and, for an old house, unglazed quarry tiles are the right choice. Ask at the DIY store for the correct treatment and cleaning method. It's not difficult, and it won't be long before they look as if they've always been there. Walls and ceiling should not be too dark, with finishes as for bedrooms. For a formal look to a plastered wall, have a dado rail at 90cm height with a darker colour below it.

baby-foot (m)	table-football	fauteuil (m)	armchair
bibliothèque (f)	library	jeux de societé (m)	board/card games
billard (m)	billiard table	lampadaire (m)	standard lamp
buffet (m)	sideboard	plante d'apartement (f)	indoor plant
canapé (m)	sofa	poêle à bois (m)	wood-burning stove
chaise (f)	dining chair	table (f)	table
chaise de bébé	high chair	table ping-pong	table-tennis table
chaise roulante	wheel chair	télé (f)	TV
extincteur (m)	fire extinguisher		

Figure 15 Dining, lounge and games room furniture

LOUNGE

Traditionally all French life revolved around the big kitchen table, and in many homes this is still the custom; there is no living-room. Many French-run B&Bs still operate this way, so it's not necessarily expected that there will be one. In fact, if you're not doing dinners or your guests are all one-night stays, I wouldn't bother. But if you're offering the total holiday experience to an international clientele, then I'm sure you will have one.

Noise is always a problem. Holiday-makers like to stay up late and it may be necessary to remind them of children asleep upstairs. If you happen to have provided a lounge a little out of the way or perhaps a north-facing room of no particular charm, it could turn out to be hardly ever used.

Furnishing

Comfortable sofas or armchairs should be provided for at least ⅔ of the guest capacity. The upholstery should have 2 sets of washable covers, and two-seater sofas are best because people don't like sitting three-in-a-row. Have some low tables that don't mind drinks being spilt on them. In addition, provide a table and chair for writing and a sideboard. Standard and table lamps can get broken; wall brackets are better. It is not difficult to collect enough paperbacks for a library, though we had to buy some second-hand French ones to keep the balance. A tiled or boarded floor with a loose mat that can be kept clear of the doors will last longer than a fitted carpet. One big indoor plant, say a ficus, makes an impact on the room, whereas small plants on the window sill just make work.

Heating

An open log fire or a stove will prove irresistible, but the room needs conventional heating as well. However, all this is expensive and you may consider closing the room when there are few guests in the winter. Instead, make some space in the dining-room which has to be heated anyway, and just have the minimum of a couple of armchairs.

Television

There is no solution to suit everyone. The British are greater addicts than the French, and other nationalities are not much interested in either country's transmissions. There are 4 possibilities:

1. No TV, especially if already provided in the bedrooms.

2. Only have French television.

3. Your own country's TV via satellite since you will have targeted clients from that country. There is an hour's time difference to the UK, so it does make the popular programmes rather late.

4. Go for as many channels as possible and let the guests sort it out for themselves.

For the record, we had French TV only; we felt that if we had British as well, then they would hog it. So actually it wasn't used much, and those who did express an opinion said they didn't need to watch on holiday. If you want satellite programmes for yourselves, the dish would have to be hidden from the guests' view or they will feel hard done by. Even if you haven't room for a large lounge, you could have a small TV room, or it could go in a games room with the implication that it's for children. Everyone will want to watch the World Cup and then it doesn't matter what language the commentary is. Have a basic remote control zapper that only changes the channels. This stops a too-clever 11-year-old improving the settings.

British sets work on the PAL system and receive British TV only via a satellite dish unless you are near the Channel. To register for reception, you have to provide a UK address. French TV uses the SECAM system, but all sets are now dual standard. It is illegal to show videos to paying guests because there is a copyright fee, though occasionally guests bring their own.

GAMES ROOM

A fitted-out room is expensive and only worth it if you have the maximum number of bedrooms and long-staying guests. There is the cost of renovating the room, the weekly cost of lighting and cleaning, and the annual cost of upkeep and maintenance. It will be well used provided it is not too isolated. If the area is an outbuilding a bit separated from the house, it would be better opened up to the outside and considered as an adjunct to outdoor living. Table-tennis is quite cheap to provide with an indoor table costing about £100. Billiards is popular but a table is expensive and very heavy, so it needs a solid floor. But it can have a lower ceiling height than table-tennis and this makes a basement room a possibility. Table-football and darts are popular too. Provide some board games and playing cards either here or in the lounge. Scrabble is the most popular and you need a French set as it's slightly different. There should be a table and chairs for playing: plastic garden furniture will do very well.

HALL

The room that visitors enter first needs to sparkle. A large display of fresh flowers is the best, but only if you have time to look after it. Otherwise, have some mirrors or brassware or a big floor-standing pot of artificial flowers (nothing twee, mind). A few B&Bs have a reception desk and a presentable one can be made from a sideboard with the back removed. But some branches of *Gîtes de France* veto this as being too much like a hotel. There must be a table or some other top for putting out the tourist information, or it could alternatively go in the lounge or dining-room. Also, the international clientele needs a good French/English dictionary handy to help the conversations along. A payphone should be here if you have one, and just inside the front door is the place for a fire extinguisher.

If your establishment caters for sports persons or hikers, they will come in with plenty of dirty boots and other equipment. Could they be relegated to a side entrance and lobby just for them?

If possible provide a downstairs toilet for casual visitors, for anyone working for you, and for elderly guests who find stairs difficult. The stairs should be well lit and ideally have a firm handrail both sides.

GUESTS' KITCHEN

If you don't do dinners, this is a good idea, but otherwise I can't see why *Gîtes de France* recommend it. No hotel has a kitchen for guests; they are supposed to patronise the restaurant. When you do provide a kitchen, it needs at least a small cooker, sink, microwave, and fridge-freezer. Have open shelves rather than cabinets for ease of cleaning and provide the usual crockery, utensils and cleaning materials. You could have a dishwasher, but in any case this is one place where there will have to be notices about leaving the room clean for others. Since the area needs table and chairs, this kitchen could be a corner of the dining-room used for breakfasts.

If there's not room for a full kitchen, how about one of the mini-kitchens available? They come as a complete unit with everything necessary except the plumbing and electricity supply. They are about 1m wide × 60cm deep, depending on the model, and that's about the size of a wardrobe.

Any provision for guests to prepare their own food or drink makes for a lot of cleaning.

STORAGE

There is never enough. A **large** linen cupboard is essential. Multiply a domestic cupboard by 3 to get an idea of the size required for half a dozen bedrooms. There should be a cleaning cupboard on each floor, and a general store somewhere on the ground floor. The size of this store will determine how much you can buy in bulk. All stores should be locked.

OFFICE

Where will you have the nerve centre for this whole enterprise? It only consists of a desk big enough for the computer and telephone, a filing cabinet and a stationery cupboard. But it needs to be somewhere to work quietly, yet be able to keep an eye on most of what is going on. Somewhere off the hall or the kitchen are the usual choices for a larger business; for the smaller establishment a desk in your own living-room would suffice, but remember there will be a lot of telephone calls.

STAFF QUARTERS

That is: yourselves. If the guests are in another building, then there's no privacy problem indoors, only in the garden. If the guests share the house with you, it depends how self-contained you want to be. If there are more than 3 bedrooms, you will probably find that number of people intrusive and really need separate accommodation. The ideal is a wing of the house for yourselves with the kitchen common to both. It is not difficult to add a stair between a downstairs sitting-room and a bedroom or two upstairs. With an outside door this will make you totally self-contained, and is easily heated if the rest of the house is closed. That's all very well for a rambling farm house; a tall town house is more difficult. You could end up with your sitting-room on the lower ground floor (euphemism for basement), and your bedroom on the second floor. I hope you thought ahead when buying the property and can manage better than this. There may be a need for a bedroom for an employee in the summer and then a room in the attic may have to suffice, provided there are some toilet facilities.

TIPS FOR MAKING IT PAY

- Have good beds.
- Have good bathrooms.
- Do not have single rooms.
- Do not have too many ornaments.

TIP FOR IMPROVING YOUR FRENCH

- Watch the television news in French.

6

Barns and Outside

SMALL OUTBUILDINGS

These are fairly easy to convert to bedrooms and should be within the scope of DIY. They need to be well done so that people don't feel they are being fobbed off, though however hard you try, they may still refer to being 'in the annex', which is slightly derogatory. If you give them their own front door and a covered terrace with garden furniture, this will make amends. When the buildings round a farm courtyard are attractively converted, the whole ensemble can look delightful. Heating and hot water are a problem with scattered buildings; you'll probably need individual electric heaters. If there are several rooms, all large enough to contain a couple of armchairs and a TV, then they are self-contained and no one need come into the house except for meals.

LARGE BARNS

Either way: you live in the barn and put the B&B in the house, or you live in the house and put the B&B in the barn – this is major construction and you need professional help. Most importantly, the barn conversion needs a carefully considered plan because, in essence, they are not very suitable for humans; they were built for animals. They have many disadvantages:

◆ They are wide and have a high roof ridge, so how are you going to provide light in the centre and what will you do with all that roof space?

◆ They were invariably part full height and part two-storey, with the ground floor of the two-storey part having a very low ceiling, just enough for cows.

◆ Both the upper and lower floor levels usually slope; that's to help the mucking out.

◆ The windows are small because they are for ventilation not for looking out.

◆ One enormous opening for farm machinery.

◆ The construction is not of the same standard as a house.

The latter is the most serious problem. Even if the old timbers are still sound, they may need strengthening or renewing; and any new load-bearing walls and posts inside will need new foundations. To tell the truth, I have never seen a really well-planned conversion of a large barn into a B&B, but I'm sure that in expert hands it can be done. The cost will be more than putting up a wholly new building. Allow **at least** a year for the actual building work even if you entrust it completely to a general contractor. If you want to organise any of it or even do some of the work yourself, better allow twice that. However at the end of the day you should have a building with a lot of character, which is what we all want for our B&B.

PARKING

If you're in a village and you haven't any on-site parking, it must be mentioned in the brochure. You will lose some custom because visitors are often carrying a lot of luggage and are loath to unload just for one night.

If you have the land, you need a gravelled parking place for each bedroom plus one or two spare. Grass won't do as it soon gets muddy. Shade is a priority so you could plant some trees, which probably won't acquire a useful size during your tenure of the property. Under cover in a barn is superb, but I really think a barn should be put to a more profitable use. Some cover is required for bicycles and motor bikes. If the parking is away from the house, people will still want to come to the front door to unload. I would have a notice about not taking responsibility for parked cars.

GARDEN

The French are not mad keen gardeners like the British, though it is increasing in popularity. Trim lawns are considered a very English thing. If you really are a keen gardener then you should have chosen the north or south west with a rainfall more like the UK. In most of the rest of the country it's not that the annual rainfall is low, it's that two month's worth comes all at once in a ten-minute storm. So for most of the summer the ground is baked dry and you'd find automatic sprinklers very expensive; in fact they're banned if there's a drought. Window-boxes in towns and plants in pots everywhere are the thing. Geraniums in summer and pansies in winter are the usual choices, but there's nothing to stop you being more individual. Hanging baskets need watering **three times a day** in very hot weather.

To find out what does succeed in a different climate and soil, look around at what is flourishing in everyone else's garden. The climate in the south is too dry for flower beds which would need watering every day, and all water is metered. Have some water butts to catch all that storm water. Shrubs are fine, but both they and trees need watering frequently for the first two years. If you have a large area, don't skimp on the ride-on mower. For about an acre a small model will do, but more than that needs a big machine – preferably with all the add-ons. Have some tables and chairs in shady spots and they will be much appreciated for picnic lunches. Then you need somewhere discreet for all the washing lines, and if there is a continuing programme of building work, it needs an area to store the mixer and materials. The entrance to the property **must** give a good first impression, so keep the path weeded and the geraniums fertilized, but otherwise reduce the gardening to what you have time for. If any areas can't be maintained, either let them go wild or grass the whole lot.

TERRACE

A paved terrace for outdoor breakfast and dinners is a great asset. The area can be gravel but paving looks better. If some of the area is covered, it can be used in the middle of the day as well, otherwise it will be too hot. Carrying the meals out of doors does make more work, but the guests love it. Provide a barbecue and lighting, together with a large table and chairs, and you have an outside room that will be used a lot.

SWIMMING POOL

Why a pool

If you're in the south and not near the sea, and you're aiming at the holiday trade, then a pool is **essential.** Even if you are near a public pool or a lake with swimming facilities, I would still have your own. The only exceptions I would make are in the mountains because walking will give quite enough exercise, and altering the contours of a mountainside for a pool is expensive; and on a working farm. But for a clientele that is merely passing through, then a pool is a luxury extra; it will increase the business a little of course. A standard pool will cost at least £20,000.

Siting

This is crucial to the enjoyment of such an expensive facility. If near the house, it looks good in the photographs, but a pool is noisy and if you stay open in the winter it will have to remain uncovered and you'll have to continue with the cleaning. A pool with its winter cover on does not look good, but keeping it uncovered is not entirely wasted effort as people do like to sit in the sunshine even when they have no intention of going in. The noise is not only children; there are late night revellers too.

A pool sited apart from the house keeps the noise away, and it can be covered in the winter. The disadvantages are that it will need extensive landscaping and, apart from aerial photos, it can't appear in the same picture as the house. This is annoying because many guide books allow only one photo. Ideally a pool should be sited on flat land to avoid the expense of retaining walls, but this is seldom possible. In any location it **must** be sheltered and away from trees.

Construction

Rectangular pool sizes:

up to 3 bedrooms	10 × 5 metres
4 to 6 bedrooms	12 × 6 metres
with other facilities	14 × 7 metres or larger

Prefabricated pools only go up to 9-metre length, but are the least expensive.

Most pools of 10 × 5m or larger are built on site with a concrete base, blockwork sides rendered, and with a plastic liner. They can be any shape or size (*see Fig. 16*).

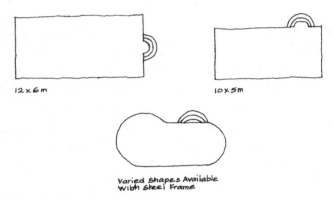

12 × 6 m   10 × 5 m

Varied Shapes Available
With Steel Frame

Figure 16   Swimming pools

There is also a patented system using corrugated steel sides, with a sand base and plastic liner, see 'Waterair' under Addresses. Good for curved shapes.

All pools have pre-cast concrete edging with paving or timber slats. Don't have gravel around the pool. Apart from being hard on the feet, you will find it being thrown into the water by children. Most pools have Roman steps, and sometimes a ladder as well. Ladders are not good for children. The usual depth is 1m at the shallow end and 2.4m at the deep end. This is not deep enough for diving, thank goodness. The filtration system can be either chlorine or salt based; the latter is much preferred by the guests. A salt system costs more to install, but it is cheaper in the long run because otehwise a pool needs a lot of chlorine but only a little salt each year. The plastic liner should last for ten years, or longer if you keep patching it. A pool with a liner should **never** be emptied or the liner will collapse.

Liners are a little slippery. It is possible to paint the inside of a pool, though I've only heard of trouble from people who have done this. For a really classy effect, a pool can be tiled. This is expensive and must be expertly done or, again, there will be trouble. In fact if you get carried away by any form of designer pool, the sky is the limit on cost and it is not compatible with making a profit on a B&B.

Extras

Don't go over the top, but a few little luxuries can surely be included in the budget. A couple of underwater lights don't cost much and it looks good in the brochure to say 'floodlit pool'. A solar shower is great fun and saves most of the sun tan oil accumulating in the water and leaving a greasy mark. The shower needs a tiled tray. Don't try and manage without a proper winter cover. An ordinary tarpaulin will lift off in the wind no matter how hard you try and weight it down. Without any cover or maintenance at all through the winter, the pool will be a dirty green soup by the spring and an enormous job to clean. Provide plenty of sun loungers and umbrellas, don't make people fight for them. They don't last long and some must be replaced every year.

Water temperature

Only the hardy will swim in a temperature below 22°C; the keen will use the pool between 22° and 24°, and the rest of humanity likes 24° at least. In most of France you should reach 22° minimum between mid June and mid September with 24°–26° for most of July and August, but it depends on location and elevation. A night cover is a chore to put on every evening but it increases the temperature by 3°. Perhaps the enthusiasts who want to swim before breakfast can be persuaded to take it off themselves. I am convinced that heating the water is the **next big thing** and I recommend you think seriously about it, preferably before building the pool. More and more people have it and you could be losing out to the competition otherwise.

Solar panels can be either on a roof or on the ground, but many are needed and they do look ugly. Alternatives are a heat pump, or even a conventional boiler. You need to get quotes for the various systems. Naturally, heating is more of an asset in the north; in the south it should increase the swimming season by a month each end, but that is when there aren't so many guests around. It needs careful consideration.

Pool house

The minimum provision is a housing for the machinery, either in an existing building or something specially built. Since people also need somewhere shady to lounge, could a barn be converted? An open-sided tent makes a pleasant place to sit, but when left up permanently it is susceptible to damage by summer storms. A real asset would be a WC by the pool; if you don't provide one where are the children to 'go'? (don't tell me).

The contractor

A large pool is beyond the scope of DIY. Get three quotes from experienced installers in the area. They will advise on the siting, get the necessary permissions, and give a ten-year guarantee on the construction. Allow at least three months for the building, and keep chivvying the builder or it will never get done in time. Constructing a pool makes an enormous disruption of the garden: be prepared. If the soil from digging the hole can be distributed on your land it will be much cheaper than taking it away, but there is a lot of it. There will be a hefty water bill in the following January.

Cleaning

Allow ½ an hour a day, 7 days a week when the pool is in use. You need an automatic vacuum cleaner plus skimmer and brushes. Take the winter cover off in mid-April to give a fortnight or more for a thorough clean, and it should be ready for use by 1st May.

Safety

You **must** put up the notice '*Beignade Non Surveillée*'. Other safety measures are shortly to be introduced, but they are not finalized yet; the pool contractor will be able to advise. They are sure to include fencing; please do something better than chain link. A stone or blockwork wall along one side is good for reflecting warmth, and may be required as a retaining wall anyway. The safety measures are to be made retrospective in 2006 to apply to all existing pools. The main sitting-out area should be outside the fence, with only 1m of paving round the pool on the inside. A security step just below water level at the deep end is helpful to hesitant swimmers, but it makes for problems with the automatic cleaner. **Do not** have an 'infinity edge'; they are not safe for children. Even with all the safety precautions you can think of, a pool is still a big worry. We had a 14-year-old dive into the shallow end and hit her head on the bottom, and a pregnant woman slipped on the steps. Fortunately neither came to any serious harm.

GROW YOUR OWN

If you do dinners, this is a lovely idea for those who have the land, the time, and the enthusiasm. As well as vegetables you should consider growing flowers for cutting, a great saving on the petty cash. If you've not got that sort of time, how about an orchard, though trees need 5–10 years before they produce much? If nothing else, at least grow your own herbs.

There are several tax advantages if you can persuade officialdom that you are an agricultural business as well as a B&B. Farmers are a protected species in France, you may have heard. It doesn't stop at tax either; you can get a bigger grant for the renovation work too. And it's not all that difficult as the definition is very wide. Basically you must have 11 hectares under cultivation **but** the following categories allow the actual areas to be increased as shown:

- Vegetables in the open air   × 5.5
- Flowers in the open air   × 15.72
- Vegetables under cloches or in unheated greenhouses   × 11
- Market gardening   × 11

If you think you could come near these areas, visit the *Chambre d'Agriculture* at your prefecture and enquire.

ANIMALS

These are absolute winners if you feel up to it. I don't mean domestic pets. In order of expense I mean donkeys, llamas, rabbits or birds in cages, fantail pigeons, ducks, fish in a tank. I'm told that chickens are almost a paying proposition, provided a fox or pack of dogs doesn't get them. Almost any animal gives the establishment a rural atmosphere.

BOULES COURT

In France perhaps this comes before a swimming pool; it's certainly a lot cheaper. It has to be absolutely flat, and is constructed of hardcore, clinker, and a topping of limestone and sharp sand, all firmly compacted with a mechanical roller. It should have an edging and old railway sleepers look better than concrete. Size 20–27.5 metres long × 2.5–4 metres wide.

CHILDREN'S AREA

A swing is the obvious first item, or perhaps a whole play apparatus with climbing rope, slide, etc. However, some people consider that swings are dangerous, and a simple log for balancing on or a climbing frame is better. **Do not** have a sand pit; it will be a lavatory for all the neighbourhood cats. To keep little children away from the main pool, you could have an inflatable plastic paddling pool just in high season.

OTHER LEISURE ACTIVITIES

Do not provide more than you can find the time to maintain properly. Broken equipment looks bad. Badminton is cheap because it is played on grass. An outdoor table-tennis table is popular and it will be used even more if it can be under cover – say, in an open barn. There's clock golf, croquet, and outdoor chess. There is even a B&B where the proprietor laid out 4 holes of golf and found it very popular, or you could have a practise net. Renting out bicycles is profitable if you know how to maintain them; hirers don't mend their own punctures. You may prefer to save on the administration and include bicycles in the free facilities.

If you fancy something outrageously expensive like a tennis court, an indoor swimming pool or a squash court, then now is your chance to put it down as a business expense. But it really must be for your own pleasure; it cannot be justified commercially for a B&B.

WOODLAND AND HEDGES

Even woodland needs maintaining. The undergrowth needs clearing and dying trees need felling otherwise they are dangerous. If the undergrowth is not dealt with, the wood will be impenetrable after five years. There are government grants for planting trees; ask at the *Chambre d'Agriculture*.

Cutting your own trees for firewood is a nice idea; oak is by far the best. Don't try and cut down a tree yourself. It takes experience to know which way it is going to fall. The usual arrangement for someone else cutting them is that if they take half the logs, the work will be done at no cost. Logs are bought in one-metre lengths, so, for all but the largest open fires, they need cutting. You will need a chain saw or electric log cutter. Logs should be stored under cover or under a tarpaulin. For seasoning two years will do, but five years are better.

There is also government help for planting hedges in the countryside. They will be mixed native species, and provided there is at least a 100-metre run they don't have to be between fields. The plants, stakes and plastic ground cover are provided at a very low cost, then you either plant the hedge yourself or help can be given, but that has to be paid for. Ask at the *Chambre d'Agriculture*.

YET MORE LAND

With land so much cheaper, you may now own more than you ever dreamed possible. If it's already let for agricultural use, then it's practically impossible to break the lease. Rents are very low and you'll be lucky to pocket a few hundred pounds. This means that you should not accept money for letting anyone use your land for any form of agriculture, or you could create a lease which will be hard to get out of. What is to be done with it? It shouldn't just be left to grow weeds. The obvious first option is to enlarge the garden and plant ornamental trees. Another idea is to let a farmer take the hay for his animals, perhaps in return for some goat's cheese? For major garden alterations it really is best to call in help with the right machinery. Trying to shift earth or clear large areas by hand is not practical.

SEPTIC TANK

You need to use an activator (as sold in supermarkets) regularly in the season and if the premises have been empty for a period. Also use some if a quantity of bleach or a caustic drain clearing product has been used. There will be a grease trap outside the kitchen, and this needs clearing at least once a year. The main tank should be emptied every 5 years. If a septic tank smells, and it has not been overloaded, then there is something wrong and it should be looked at by a specialist.

RUBBISH

This is one dirty big problem because there is so much of it. If doing dinners, you need one domestic-size bin for each bedroom plus one for yourselves. I hope there is a collection in your area, but even then you have to take it to the roadside. If there is no collection, then you are faced with taking it to the nearest public bin. In this case you could ask at the town hall if there is a commercial arrangement. Bottle banks have existed for many years and you will collect a great many, so you need to provide some containers. More and more communes now expect you to sort the rubbish into various re-cyclable categories and, with the quantities produced, you will find this a real chore. The enclosure should be kept clean to avoid insects; should not have food left in loose bags to attract rats; and should be dog proof to avoid rubbish spread all over the garden one day. There will always be a public tip in your area which you are entitled to use for large items.

TIPS FOR MAKING IT PAY

- In the country have a pool to encourage long-stay visitors.
- Have a terrace for outdoor meals.
- Don't try and make an English garden.
- Have a variety of outdoor occupations.

arbre (m)	tree	ordure (f)	rubbish
arbuste (m)	shrub	parc (m)	estate
arroser	to water	parking (m)	car park
arrosoir (m)	watering can	paysagiste (m)	landscape gardener
badminton (m)	badminton	pergola (f)	pergola
bain de soleil (m)	sun lounger	piscine (f)	swimming pool
balançoire (f)	garden swing	plante (f)	plant
bois (m)	woodland	plante grimpante	climbing plant
boulodrome (m)	boules court	plate-bande (f)	flower bed
brouette (f)	wheelbarrow	portail (m)	entrance gate
bulbe (m)	bulb	portique (m)	play equipment
champ (m)	field	potager (m)	vegetable garden
clôture (f)	fence	poubelle (f)	rubbish bin
court (m)	tennis court	prairie (f)	meadow
déchetterie (f)	public tip	remorque (f)	car trailer
dépendence (f)	outbuilding	salon de jardin (f)	garden furniture
engrais (m)	fertilizer	store (m)	awning
fleur (f)	flower	terrain (m)	land
gazon (m)	lawn	terrasse (f)	terrace
grange (f)	barn	terreau (m)	compost
graine (f)	seed	tondeuse (f)	lawn mower
gravier (m)	gravel	tondeuse auto-portée	ride on mower
haie (f)	hedge	tri (m)	sorting of rubbish
herbe (f)	grass	vélo (m)	bicycle
jardin (m)	garden	vélo tout terrain (VTT)	mountain bike
jardinier (m)	gardener	verger (m)	orchard
mauvaise herbe (f)	weed		

Figure 17 Glossary

TIP FOR IMPROVING YOUR FRENCH

◆ Read a French magazine such as *Paris Match* or *Le Nouvel Observateur*.

7

The Table

BREAKFAST

For *chambres d'hôtes* the law requires that breakfast is included in the room price, and this must be stated in the tariff. If you are enrolling in *Gîtes de France* they will require you to set up a sample breakfast for their inspection of the premises. Of course they will expect to see a continental breakfast; but, even so, it should be copious.

Time

A few proprietors have one fixed time for breakfast and this is not liked. We said between 7.45 and 10.00 which seemed OK. Occasionally people wanted to make an earlier start and then we left them something.

Beverage

We offered orange juice plus a choice of tea, coffee, decaffeinated coffee, hot chocolate and herb tea. The French like their tea weak by our standard and without milk (they believe strong tea is bad for the nerves), so always provide a jug of hot water. The coffee should be freshly percolated: either give a fresh pot to people as they arrive or have insulated jugs. Children like hot chocolate; a few adults do too, so you'll have to learn how to make it and it is served in large cups. For herb, tea *verveine* (verbena) is the most popular. Fresh milk is hard to come by every day so we used long life. Note that granulated sugar is for cooking; lump sugar is for the table.

Bread and cake

Everyone has the mental picture of crusty bread and buttery croissants – a dream that is becoming ever harder to fulfil as small bakers are closing by the hundred every year. We did collect fresh bread by car every morning, but the shop wasn't open every day in winter and it's a chore when there are only two guests. When fresh bread wasn't available it's best to freeze the *pain de campagne* (country loaf), then de-frost it in a microwave, sprinkle with water, and pop it in a hot oven for 10 minutes. An alternative is to buy the part-baked bread, but this is expensive. Or you could bake your own in one of those machines, but that's also expensive and it doesn't make a French-shaped loaf.

Always buy good butter croissants; the large supermarket packs are poor. Croissants can also be frozen and freshened up in the oven, though of course it's not quite so good. As an alternative, you can have *pain au raisin* (Chelsea buns), and children like *pain au chocolat*. As well as ordinary bread, put out some *brioche* (a light milk bread), and either *biscottes* or *pains grillés* (both these are pre-toasted bread). Lean heavily on your baker for an account and a 10 per cent discount; you'll be buying a lot. The French prefer their butter unsalted.

For a French breakfast, think 'tea time' because they really do have bread and butter and jam, and cake. Well, only occasionally cake, and by '*cake*' they mean 'fruit cake'. Home-made is wonderful only if you've got the time, which I didn't have, as I tried it once and it wasn't popular with other nationalities.

Jam

But I did make all the jam. Really it's not that difficult, but you need a lot. One trouble is that many fruits ripen in high season, and some of the taste is lost if they are frozen for making up later. Honey is popular too, but the French do not like the English-style chunky marmalade, so it wasn't always put out.

Plum is the cheapest jam to make; strawberry and apricot are the most popular. These fruits can be bought in bulk in the market. Quince jelly will be new to many and sounds very rural. The British staple of blackberry and apple is not possible due the lack of blackberries (not enough rain) and lack of suitable apples (they don't have Bramleys). Oranges (Seville oranges) for marmalade are only available in the larger markets. Use ordinary granulated sugar, except for strawberries which must either have the special jam-making sugar or a setting agent. Many French still make their own jam and the big preserving pans are widely available. The country folk have a gas ring in an outhouse for making preserves. You could do the same and make vast quantities and sell some to the guests – you'll have to judge whether it really is profitable. Use the paraffin wax sold for food use for sealing the jars and you'll never be bothered with ants.

It looks generous to put 4 varieties of home-made jam on the table, and when one day a man came into the kitchen to compliment me on my apricot jam, it made the all effort seem worthwhile.

Other foods

The breakfast glossary (*Fig. 18*) contains the basics for a continental breakfast, but you may like to provide more. You can offer boiled eggs, fresh fruit or yoghourt (not the cheapest, please). Breakfast cereals are considered to be children's food, so it's optional if you include any; they should be decanted into containers. It really isn't necessary to do the big English cooked meal even if they are the only nationality present. **Do not** have the hotel-type butters and jams in little packs.

At grade 4 level, the breakfast should include all of the above plus sliced cold meats and cheese in the northern European style.

Laying on a copious breakfast means that a few people will squirrel away something for their lunch. They think they are getting something for nothing. They aren't. In fact it's the other way round; you are benefiting

French	English	French	English
assiette (f)	plate	maison	home-made
beurre (m)	butter	nappe (f)	tablecloth
beurre doux	unsalted butter	œuf (m)	egg
boulangerie (f)	bakery	œuf en coque	hard boiled egg
café (m)	coffee	pain (m)	bread
café décaféiné	decafinated coffee	pain de compagne	country bread
café soluble	instant coffee	pain au raisin	Chelsea bun
cafetière (f)	coffee pot	petit-déjeuner (m)	breakfast
cake (m)	fruit cake	petit pain (m)	bread roll
chocolat (m)	drinking chocolate	pichet (m)	jug
confiture (f)	jam, marmalade	porcelaine (f)	china
couteau (m)	knife	serviette (f)	napkin
cuillère (f)	spoon	soucoupe (f)	saucer
cuillère à café	tea spoon	sucre (m)	sugar
jus d'orange (m)	orange juice	sucre en morceaux	lump sugar
lait (m)	milk	sucrier (m)	sugar bowl
lait demi-écrémé	semi-skimmed milk	tasse (f)	cup
lait écrémé	skimmed milk	thé (m)	tea
lait entier	full cream milk	théière (f)	teapot
lait frais	fresh milk	tisane (f)	herb tea
lait UHT	long life milk	yaourt (m)	yoghourt

Figure 18 Glossary for breakfasts

from their warm feeling for the few cents cost of an apple. So go all out to encourage it.

TABLE D'HOTE

The words *table d'hôte* have no exact translation into English. The Larousse dictionary defines it as: *table servie à heures fixes et à tant par tête* (meals served at fixed hours at so much per head), which seems a fair description. But it's difficult for us foreigners to know quite what standard to aim for. The answer is that it should be good home cooking, such as you would serve to friends and family on a slightly formal occasion. Bear in mind that in France this means a convivial meal of at least 4 courses with wine, but it need not be as formal as a good restaurant.

Offering dinners is a very big decision because it is so much work. It can take nearly as much time as all the rest put together. We didn't have a *table d'hôte* for the first three years, then when we added it the business increased greatly. Many people will only stay where they can have dinner, so you get more clients for the B&B as well as the profit on the meals. If you're in a village with a couple of restaurants within walking distance, there's no imperative to do dinners. In the country with no restaurant near then you will have to do dinners. It is reckoned that a *table d'hôte* increases the occupancy by at least 20 nights a year, that it doubles the income per room, **but** that it can take up as much as 50 per cent of your time. Think carefully about the commitment.

The reasons for eating at a *table d'hôte* are:

◆ Reluctance to go out again after a long journey
◆ Liking a drink with the meal
◆ Not wanting to take children to a restaurant
◆ Wanting to put children to bed at a reasonable hour
◆ Looking forward to the good cooking promised in the brochure

Though keen cooks, neither of us had any commercial experience, and we did find the dinners very hard work. From mid-June to mid-September we were doing four to twelve dinners a day, seven days a week, with only a handful of days in about 14 weeks when no-one wanted to eat in. It wasn't possible to take turns either, as it takes two to cook, serve and clear up. I hope I've not painted too daunting a picture; there are ways to lighten the load, and there were rewards apart from the obvious one that it's profitable. Notwithstanding their anti-British prejudice we found that the French eat in more than the other nationalities. After all, the local restaurants are no novelty for them and they are suspicious of eating where they have no reliable recommendation. The sound of a table full of guests all chatting away, sometimes in two or even three languages, was very gratifying. And the compliments received made it seem very worthwhile.

PROFIT

A hotelier told me that a restaurant price should consist of one third the cost of the ingredients, one third overheads, and one third profit. Hmm . . . I don't think we came near this with such small numbers. We found about ⅔ of our guests had dinner, but this varies a lot between establishments. Gîtes de France insists that you quote a B&B price and a dinner price separately **or** a demi-pension or pension price. In fact it's illegal to insist on people having dinner by only quoting pension prices. We found that even people in our *gîte* had dinner occasionally. Out of season we were often doing a meal for 2 and that doesn't pay unless the price is very high; we reckoned it needed 6 to see much of a profit. A *table d'hôte* has a **fixed price** and does not have a choice of menus, but you may offer a gourmet meal at an increased price. Look through the brochures and see what other people are charging. You will find it's a lot less than restaurant prices in the UK.

LIGHTEN THE LOAD

There are a few possibilities. The first is to hire help for the evenings, but it would have to be a flexible arrangement because, even in high season, the number at the table can vary from none to a full house. The duties would be to lay the table, serve, clear away, load the dishwasher, wash up and tidy the kitchen, sweep the dining-room floor and lay the breakfast. At least then the chef could leave off work as soon as the main course is served. You need to pay only a little over the minimum wage for this, but if you hire someone to do the actual cooking they will want more.

Another way is not to serve dinner every day. Check that the local restaurants aren't closing the same day. There are several disadvantages to this. Firstly, once your customers have eaten out, they may continue to do so, and you lose business. Secondly, you have got to warn people when they book, because they never read the brochure closely. And lastly, it is difficult to have a demi-pension reduction.

Alternatively you could only do dinners in high season when there will be a full table. At the opposite end of the scale is the host with only 1 or 2 bedrooms who offers dinner only on the day of arrival; if you regularly invite some friends as well it could be fun, though you won't make much.

If you don't do dinners at all, how about negotiating with a restaurant for a 10 per cent off voucher for your guests' first night? Most establishments would go along with this. You'd have to mention it in your brochure and make some arrangements for booking.

DEMI-PENSION

It is expected that there will be a reduction for stays of a few days with dinners. *Gîtes de France* recommend 3 days, but 5 or 7 days are also common. You don't have to, and it makes for problems, mainly in that it commits you to cooking every single day. If you do want to take one day a week off, or go to some special event, what will you charge if a meal is not available? Or you'll have to make some alternative arrangements. Nevertheless, demi-pension does help to fill the table, and if you want to make money doing meals, you have got to work hard at keeping up the numbers.

CHILDREN

It is also expected that there will be a good reduction for children, say aged 2 to 10, but you may choose other ages. For the under 2s it is not usual to charge anything, but you will be expected to heat up the baby food and bottles in the microwave. The parents provide the baby food, though you should keep something for emergencies. Some B&Bs have a separate children's meal – say, at 7 o'clock. If served out of doors, it saves a lot of clearing up. It needs to be supervised and probably one of the parents would be willing. This arrangement needs to be confirmed with the parents, because some French people prefer their children to eat at the adult table even if it is not till 8 o'clock. In this case small children may be put to bed after the main course. The children's menu need only have 2 courses and a drink, so you don't have to charge much. When they eat at the adult table, you just have to rely on them having only a little.

THE HOSTS

Gîtes de France **insist** that the proprietors eat with the guests to give a family atmosphere. Very few do. There are several reasons why this is an impractical idea:

1. Many women are too conscious of their figure to want such a large meal every day.

2. The cook will use a very limited range of recipes week in week out.

3. With more than 6 guests it needs 2 staff to cope.

4. If the dishes aren't cleared up as the meal progresses, you'll be up till all hours.

5. A partial solution is that one of you could join the guests while the other cooks.

   We tried, when possible, to join the table for coffee.

So when do you eat? I'm afraid that in high season you'll be snatching your meals whenever you can. You should be able to have lunch in peace.

LUNCH

You must be gluttons for punishment. Of course you would only be offering lunch if you are a *table d'hôte*. In fact it's a rare B&B that does lunches, simply because it's seldom asked for unless you are really remote. However, you could offer a packed lunch, which can either be taken away or eaten in a shady spot in your own grounds. Or you could do a salad. If you are offering full board it must be made clear that it is only a light meal, because the midday lunch is still the main meal of the day for some French people.

If you don't offer lunches, what are people to do if staying more than one night? Our guests' usual pattern was to go out in the morning, eat out or have a picnic, return mid-afternoon to spend the rest of the day by the pool, and then eat in. Families with young children, and the occasional couple, do sometimes stay around all day and bought their own picnic. We had a large fridge/freezer for the guests' use. If you provide any form of mini kitchen or barbecue, then it will be used for lunches.

REGIONAL COOKING

French cuisine has a world-wide reputation, so it is with some trepidation that I, an Englishwoman, dare to put down a few words on the subject, the more so as their opinion of my country's cooking is rock bottom as exemplified by the following story. An English B&B proprietor asked her

French guests if they wanted dinner that night. 'Oh no,' they said, 'we know the English can't cook'. Naturally I don't accept that opinion. In fact the French need to look to their laurels because high wages are closing restaurants at a rapid rate and the spread of giant hypermarkets is affecting home cooking. Nevertheless the French will expect a good standard at a *table d'hôte*. They think of food in terms of taste rather than nutrition, and will take a keen interest in all that is put in front of them. You will be asked detailed questions like, 'How many eggs in the *crème caramel?*' This will be in contrast to the seeming indifference of the British with their 'very nice', or Americans with their over the top enthusiasm.

Gîtes de France **insist** that the cooking must be 'regional'. This is a concept unknown in the British Isles, whatever the tourist boards say. So you really ought to make the effort to learn some recipes from your region. You may well be at a loss to know what gastronomic region you are in and what the local cuisine is. I'm sure your local bookshop will have a shelf of cook books, but here is a rough guide to get you started thinking along the right lines.

Regional cooking derives from the climate, and the country can be divided approximately into four areas according to the type of fat used:

◆ Butter – the largest area, including Paris and the north (with the exception of Alsace-Lorraine), the Atlantic coast, and the east. All areas with a climate suitable for raising cattle. This is the *haute cuisine* so famous all over the world.

◆ Lard – mostly pigs and geese; the animals of the poor because they can be raised economically. Alsace-Lorraine where the pig dominates; and the centre and south centre down to the Mediterranean where the goose dominates. This is the least well-known cuisine.

◆ Olive oil – the south east where olives will grow in the poor soil. This is a variation of the Mediterranean cooking we know so well.

◆ Butter, Lard and Oil – the Pyrénées. A mixture of all three because the Pyrenean mountains stretch from the Atlantic to the Mediteranean and contain many formerly isolated valleys, each of which developed its own specialities.

DINNER (*see Fig. 19*)

Chambres d'Hôtes Bon Temps
****
****

TABLE D'HOTE
Dîner 18€ (enfants 9€) à 20 heures

Potage/Entrée
Plat du Jour
Fromage
Dessert Maison
¼ l vin & café compris

Uniquement sur réservation
avant 10 heures le matin

Figure 19   The normal number of courses for dinner

Entrée
Keep it simple. Learn a few soups and salads. Soup should be ladled out at the table so as not to spill it. Salads can be either on the plate or a selection in the centre of the table.

Main course
Practise 7 recipes over the winter. In the rare event that anyone books demi-pension for a fortnight they won't be taken aback if the same thing appears again. Don't ignore rabbit; it's very popular in France. So are kidneys, but some British don't like offal so don't serve them unless you've confirmed first that it's acceptable. In French cooking the vegetables and the

potatoes/rice/pasta are minor accompaniments to the meat and fish. The vegetable element of the meal is provided by salads, and the starch by bread.

Cheese
This is served before the dessert. The French will know the prices of the various types, so go for the middle of the range. Do them the honour of only having French cheeses. No need to have too many. For 2 people, have 2 varieties, for 3 or 4 people have 3 varieties, for 5 and up have a maximum of 4 varieties; with a good mix of hard, soft, goat's and blue cheeses. Avoid *Emmental*, that's for cooking; and *raclette,* that's for serving hot as a dip at parties. Either put the cheese on a board, English fashion, or go round serving it as in restaurants. Cheese should be removed from the fridge half an hour before use. A lot of the cost is in the wastage, so wrap each piece in foil for storing. Cheese is accompanied by bread or rolls, **not** biscuits, and **no** butter.

Dessert
Learn the French standards which are:

> *Crème caramel*
> *Mousse au chocolat*
> *Tarte aux pommes*

and two more which are not quite so common:

> *Îles flottantes*
> *Tarte tatin*

However I found that not everyone wants a pie in a 4-course meal, so I didn't do one very often. Don't worry about buying the pastry; everyone does. Although the rest of the meal should be French-style, you can be more international with the desserts. Tiramasu has had its day, and now the current **in** dessert is *crumble au pomme* (apple crumble). You would find buying the fancy ice creams and frozen gateaux expensive. If you really don't want to have cheese and a dessert, there's a hybrid which consists of serving *confiture de cerises* (cherry jam) with *fromage de brébis* (sheep's milk cheese).

More than once I was asked to provide a birthday cake. So I made a gateau, and added candles if it was for a child. This, of course, was at no extra cost; one has to do the little bit extra.

Coffee

Freshly made real coffee of course, and served in a *demi-tasse* (small cup). For those who say they can't sleep after drinking coffee, you may have to provide tea, herb tea, or decaffeinated coffee. Some British will ask for milk. Since there isn't room for milk in a *demi-tasse*, the solution is to put a small jug of light cream on the table. The 'cash and carries' sell large packs of the little chocolates if you want them.

Drinks

We tried an aperitif (kir) but found people weren't very interested, so gave it up. You may have a different experience.

In France you **must** serve wine with dinner. Allow ¼-litre per person of an ordinary red table wine. Chill a bottle of white just in case anyone asks for it. Start by buying a *vin ordinaire* in a 5-litre cube at the supermarket until you get acquainted with what is available locally. Then, if you are in a wine-growing area, buy in bulk at a vineyard or local *cave* (wine merchant's). At a vineyard **always** try a sample, and don't buy too cheaply. We found the French to be modest drinkers at the table; I regret to say it's the Brits who often drink a lot. Well, it's 'free' if it's included in the price of the meal, isn't it? This poses a dilemma, because what will you do if they ask for some more? One solution is to allow them to bring their own wine to the table, otherwise just give them a little more for the sake of goodwill.

Red wine should be served 'at room temperature'. Yes, but what temperature is that? In fact modern central heating and very hot weather are **too warm**. So keep it in a cool room, not the fridge, until required. White wine should be served 'cool'. Yes, but not **too cool**. It will take 2 hours in a fridge to reach drinking temperature, or 3 hours if the door is opened frequently. If you're in a hurry, it can be cooled in an ice bucket in 10–20 minutes if the bucket is filled with ice and water up to the neck of the bottle. Tip the bottle upside down for a few minutes if it is not quite covered.

The above is assuming you have not taken up a full drinks licence. I would get the *table d'hôte* running first and see how it goes, before expanding. Certainly you could make more, but there are obstacles. One is your application could be strongly opposed by local hoteliers; another is *Gîtes de France* may consider you to be too much like a hotel, and lastly there's security for the stock.

Obviously you must put water on the table but, apart from the cost, there are differing opinions on the merits of tap water and bottled mineral water. Some think tap water is not pure enough; others that water 'straight out of a plastic bottle' is suspect. You'll have your own opinion.

amuse-gueule (m)	cocktail snack	dîner (m)	dinner
apéritif (m)	aperitif	entrée (f)	starter
assiette creuse (f)	soup plate	fourchette (f)	fork
boîte (f)	tin can	fromage (m)	cheese
bougie (f)	candle	louche (f)	ladle
bouilloire (f)	kettle	poêle (f)	frying pan
carafe (f)	decanter	plat (m)	dish
casserole (f)	saucepan	plat du jour	dish of the day
chandelier (m)	candle stick	plat principal	main course
conserve (f)	tinned food	potage (m)	soup
couvert (m)	place setting	régime (m)	diet
cuillère à soup (f)	soup spoon	sel & piovre	salt & pepper pots
demi-tasse (f)	coffee cup	soupière (f)	soup-tureen
dessert (m)	dessert	surgelés (m)	frozen food
digestif (m)	after dinner drink	verre (m)	drinking glass

It would take a book to give all the foods used in cooking.
In fact there is such a book, 'The Traveller's French Food & Drink' (see Appendix for details).

Figure 20 Glossary for dinners

Some small further points on dinners:

◆ Give generous portions.

◆ Have meals out of doors if at all possible.

◆ Getting the food to the table hot is absolutely essential. This is not helped by the British etiquette of not starting before everyone is served.

◆ Don't forget to put bread on the table.

Traditionally the French keep the same plate and cutlery throughout the meal. It's polite to finish everything and wipe the plate clean with a piece of bread, unlike Americans where it's polite to leave some. Dishwashing machines mean we are now more lavish with the utensils, but you could tell guests to keep the cutlery from the entrée to the main course, it gives a French feel to the meal and does save on the quantity needed.

DIETS

You will receive many and varied requests. For vegetarians you need to have one dish in the repertoire. It should not be an omelette because only too often that is the only option. If a vegetarian wants demi-pension, don't be a martyr, just say it's not possible. For a diabetic dessert, arrange sliced fruits in a pattern on a large plate; it looks great.

For people with allergies, just do your best. It would help a lot if one had advance warning of special requirements, but that doesn't always happen.

BARBECUE

I do recommend having a barbecue once a week, say Sundays, in high season. We found it very popular. It was the one time when we did eat with our guests, and since the people in our *gîte* invariably came as well, it made for a good crowd. Profitable too, as the food is fairly cheap. Due to the climate, it was only rained off once. We set it slightly earlier at 7pm, and our menu was:

Aperitif (kir or white wine)
Barbecued meats with a buffet
   of salads
One large round of cheese } second and third helpings encouraged
Big bowl of fruit salad
Coffee
Light red wine (½ litre per person)

You may feel that with a barbecue in the evening, a brunch would be appropriate. This poses all sorts of problems of charging, and timing, and when do you get in the bedrooms, such that I don't see it working.

Have you thought of not doing the barbecue yourselves, and getting some friends to do it? They wouldn't need cooking experience. Then you take the evening off.

GOURMET DINNER

Gourmet Dinner/Candlelit Dinner In The Barn/*Le 14 juillet* – any excuse will do if you want to put on something special, and of course charge more. Proviso no.1 – do you have the skill? Proviso no. 2 – how are you going to charge extra to people who have booked demi-pension? I did warn that demi-pension has its problems. Unless you are an expert chef, it would be very difficult to do an ordinary dinner as well as a special. You need to go to some good restaurants to find what to serve, but remember that your drinks **have** to be included in the price unless you have a full licence. The wines should be *Appellation d'Origine Contrôlée/AOC*, i.e. good. A problem with a candlelit dinner is that in the summer it doesn't get dark till late.

I would be very careful about doing a 'foreign night'. The French are not keen on other cuisines, and the only ones found occasionally are Vietnamese and Moroccan.

Have you thought of hiring someone else to cook your gourmet dinner? It would need an experienced person and they will want paying. Whether hiring help or not, be careful with the price to make sure you are making a profit.

CHRISTMAS AND NEW YEAR

You may like to do a special meal for these occasions, but the difficulty is in the advertising to ensure a full house. You'd have to remember to include it in all your regular advertisements which are sent to the guide books nearly 18 months in advance, and in your brochure. It would be very embarrassing to end up with only 2 guests. But a full house would be an immense amount of work, so are you sure?

You are unlikely to attract any French for Christmas, as it's not an important festival, so you will be doing the full English if at all; which needs no elaboration here.

Since we have no particular tradition for the New Year, I would go for a French meal. In this case it **must** start with oysters and champagne and there should be about 6 courses. There should be several good wines, and a *digestif* to finish/ toast the New Year. Apart from the quality of the food and the conversation, the French judge the success of a meal by the number of courses and the length of time spent at the table. To make the occasion a good 4-hour affair you could introduce an event between each course, for instance: a game at the table/poetry reading/music/Queen's speech at Christmas or a suitable reading/singalong. I've had such an occasion recounted to me and told it was a great success.

Again, be careful with the price to make sure you are making a profit. You would have to decide whether these events are to be a family event or whether you want to make money. For making money you can't have too many free-loading relatives and friends unless they are really going to work hard.

FROZEN FOOD

The French are very censorious about frozen food from the aspect of both taste and safety. You are **not allowed to freeze animal products** except with proper fast freezing equipment, which is unlikely in a B&B. In fact, they put great emphasis on produce being fresh, so you should not even serve frozen vegetables unless home grown. There is no restriction on products bought already frozen, which can be a life saver, since you need to have an emergency supply of practically everything for the day when all hell breaks loose.

RESERVATION

Some people think a *table d'hôte* is a restaurant and meals can be ordered when you sit down at the table. We **never** offered dinner unless the reservation was made before 10am. We certainly lost business this way, and the reservation requirement had to be emphasized to clients when they booked. If you feel you can cope with last-minute orders, all well and good. You'd need to rely a lot on the freezer, and if everyone is at the same table, the late arrivals will be having a different menu. This happens all the time in a restaurant of course. Another way is always to cook 2 extra portions; it would probably pay if your business is largely one-night stays.

THE CHEF

Don't be overawed by the thought of the cooking. It's not like having a dinner party every night. Of course it does help to have started with only 2 or 3 bedrooms and learnt to cope with greater numbers as you go along. One great problem for amateurs is that they are not quick enough. But speed will improve; once you have done the dish twelve times it gets a lot easier. Just wait for the day when you get the back-handed compliment: 'Now we know the English can cook!,' and you will feel you have done something to dispel our poor reputation.

TEA

As long as guests arrived before 6pm we offered them a cup of tea or coffee (or beer on a hot day), together with home-made shortbread (there's a homely touch), and a fruit juice for the children. It made a good opportunity for a little chat. The French sometimes refused as afternoon tea is not their custom. After 6.00 we were too busy in the kitchen.

Many guests would like a drink in the afternoon yet you have quite enough to do without being 'on duty' all the time. If there is no tea making facility in the bedroom it is a good idea to have a beverage trolley in the lounge, with a kettle and everything in packet form. Keeping it clean and topped up is all more work of course.

Last thing at night some French like a *tisane* (herbal tea). It is believed to promote a good night's sleep, rather like the Ovaltine and Horlicks of a couple of generations back. Leave the necessary facilities on the landing; they should include sugar but not milk. I came across the *tisane* somewhere I stayed and rather liked it. It's these little touches that mean so much.

TIPS FOR MAKING IT PAY

◆ Keep a careful watch on the costs of each portion of food.

◆ Serve meals out of doors if possible; it's such a novelty that people concentrate less on what they're eating.

◆ Let people make their own hot drinks.

TIP FOR IMPROVING YOUR FRENCH

◆ Buy a French recipe book and try out some new dishes.

(Note that the French measurements *cuillère à café* and *cuillère à soup* are the English tea spoon and table spoon).

8

Finance and Administration

FINANCE

To buy a property substantial enough for a B&B, most purchasers under 50 will need a mortgage, even though transferring from the high priced UK to lower priced France. Whether this is so or not, there could be extensive restoration necessary, and the funds may have to be borrowed. Make out a detailed financial plan which should allow for very little B&B income in the first two years. It should include furnishing and equipment and some advertising. How does it look? Have you got enough capital or do you need a loan?

The easiest loan to obtain will always be a mortgage on the property. There are no building societies in France; mortgages are from banks. Provided you don't want more than 50 per cent and can cope with a 10-year repayment period, there should be no difficulty. Mortgages for 25 years are hard to get anyway. If asking for more than 50 per cent the bank will enquire into your personal income, otherwise they might not trouble you. There will be fees both to the *notaire* and the bank for setting it up, but there is seldom a penalty for early repayment. The process should be faster than the UK because they are not waiting around for a favourable survey. The monthly payments will be taken direct from your account and they will insist on insurance. You could always ask to increase the mortgage later on for further improvements or a swimming pool. Naturally, if you default, the property will be repossessed and sold at auction, probably for a lower figure than an estate agent would achieve.

Some British banks and building societies will lend on foreign properties, though they will want a survey and may not be too happy about you disappearing from their shores.

Obviously you mustn't have too much debt, but don't struggle on without any. You'll get the business on a profitable footing much faster by borrowing some money for improvements, rather than waiting to save it. The interest is allowable as a business expense.

GRANTS

Grants for renovation are only available to members of *Gîtes de France* and *Clévacances*. A typical grant will be for 30 per cent of the building work with a maximum of £2,000 (in 2002) per bedroom. But the amounts and conditions vary between *départements*, so make enquiries at an early stage. You may be able to get additional money for architects' fees, improvements to the environment, or extra facilities such as a swimming pool. It is not possible to get a grant for a new building or for the furnishing. You have to submit quotations in a particular format with the application, so ask for details before speaking to builders; and the approval will take some time. The documents are sent to the *Conseil Général* (local authority) for scrutiny, and if you are in a hurry to begin the work, you can try applying to them direct for permission to start ahead of the formal approval. It is also possible for the grant to cover the cost of materials for doing the work yourself. The money will not be released until the rooms are furnished ready for use and inspected, so you have to fund it yourself until then. With the letter of approval in hand, your bank will probably look favourably on a loan. These grants are well worth having, but since they are taxed as income, try to get the money in the earlier years when you aren't making much. There are extra grants for farmers and historic buildings.

FORMING A COMPANY

There are fiscal advantages in trading as a company, and if the business is substantial it is worth investigating, though it is best done at the time of buying the property rather than later.

The *Société á Responsabilité Limité /SARL* is the most usual for a husband and wife working from home. It is similar to the UK limited company. But there are many other forms of company and the best person to advise is the *notaire*.

It is possible to register the business in the UK if you have a British-based partner and address. This will avoid some items of French legislation. Take advice from an international lawyer.

PRICES

The basic source of income is the room charge, generally quoted for two people. Buy several guide books and make a thorough survey of what others with similar accommodation to your own are charging, and fix yours in the middle. **Do not** down grade yourself – possibly your establishment has some special features. And **do not** start low with the intention of raising the price later; it alienates existing customers. However, don't be afraid to raise it a little each year; it's so easy to let it drift, and people will expect an increase anyway.

An analysis of the prices charged by *Gîtes de France* members in 2003 in one *département* gives the following figures:

	3 épis	*4 épis*
bed & breakfast	€45 (110 members)	€82 (9 members)
dinner	€15 (49 members)	€22 (9 members)

You will see that less than half the *3 épis* level had *table d'hôte*, whereas all the *4 épis* members had *table d'hôte*. It's always the case that the two price levels do overlap.

Where a range of prices was given, the highest has been used; and you will see they are lower than is found in the UK. This is why some British proprietors opt for a wholly foreign clientele and it is achieved by not being in any French guides. You will have to weigh up the advantages. It only works if you have a high-standard establishment, and you will certainly lose some out-of-season business. Bearing in mind that you will, in any case, be aiming for an international clientele, the following example of a tariff (*see Fig. 21 – English; Fig. 22 – French*) shows slightly above-average prices for *3 épis*.

Chambres d'Hôtes BonTemps

TARIFF 2004

Room charge per night	Jun, Jul, Aug, Sep	Other months
One person	€45	€32
Two people	€58	€45
Three people	€73	€60

All rooms have a private bathroom
Generous continental breakfast included

Babies aged 0–2 free
Cot and high chair are available

Children aged 3–10 €10 (in room with 2 adults)

Meals: Lunch €8 . . . 2 courses with beverage or picnic hamper
Dinner €18 . . . 4 courses with ¼ lt table wine and coffee
Children aged 3–10: Lunch €4, Dinner €9

Pension & Demi-pension (minimum 3 nights) − 10%

Reservation: €10 per room per night or €15 for pension and demi-pension
The reservation fee will be refunded if cancellation is received at least 8 weeks before arrival

Also 2 self-catering cottages for 4 people . . . please ask for tariffs

---

Figure 21 Price list which can be inserted into a brochure

You should also ascertain what the hotels in your area are charging. You will find that the ordinary sort of town centre hotel is really a restaurant with a few rooms to let and no other facilities for guests. They make their

---

Chambres d'Hôtes BonTemps

TARIFF 2004

Chambre par nuit	juin, juillet août, sept	autres mois
1 personne	45€	32€
2 personnes	58€	45€
3 personnes	73€	60€

Toutes nos chambres ont salle de bain privatif
Petit déjeuner copieux compris

Bébés de 0 à 2 ans gratuits
Lit pour bébé et chaise haute disponibles

Enfants de 3 à 10 ans 10€ dans une chambre avec 2 adultes

Repas Déjeuner 8€ . . . 2 plats avec boisson ou Panier pique-nique
Dîner 18€ . . . 4 plats, ¼ lt vin & café compris
Enfants de 3 à 10 ans: Déjeuner 4€, Dîner 9€

Pension & Demi-pension (minimum 3 nuits) — 10%

Réservation 10€ par nuit par chambre ou 15€ pour pension & demi-pension
L'acompte sera remboursée si l'annulation est faite plus de 8 semaines avant l'arrivée

Aussi 2 gîtes indépendants pour 4 personnes . . . demandez nos tarifs

---

Figure 22 Price list which can be inserted into a brochure

money from the restaurant, so their charge will be low. Yours should be higher than this, even though you are 'only' a B&B, and remember, they will not be including breakfast. A local 3-star hotel in its own grounds is a different matter and you will probably like to be a little below this unless you have a very special building.

There is no doubt that the British appreciate the price being quoted in sterling. The trouble is the exchange rate on the euro does vary and you will end the year with different prices. So far it has only moved a little, but it does niggle some customers if they find out and it is not in their favour. The prices for the year must be fixed by July of the previous year for entry in the guide books, so you are faced with forecasting world currency movements a long way ahead. Alternatively, you can always accept payment in sterling even if the prices are quoted in euros. For an up-to-date tourist exchange rate, go to:- **www.travelex.co.uk**

With 1 or 2 bedrooms you could claim there are practically no extra costs and you are only charging your time, so the cost can be low. This is not realistic because you have put at the guests' disposal the entire establishment of your home which costs a great deal. Sometimes a family turns up and begs you to take them in, even with mattresses on the floor, anything. You sympathise, but be careful. What will you charge when you have been put to a lot of trouble, but it still ends up with a sub-standard service? Discuss prices **before** you agree.

FILLING THE ROOMS

The first twelve months are tough and not many B&Bs achieve an occupancy greater than 10 per cent for the year. This will come as a blow if the finances are already overstretched and you were confidently expecting 65 per cent, as one couple were. This 10 per cent won't even pay the costs, so you need to budget for a loss in the first year. After that you **must aim for a 30 per cent occupancy** for the year before you can feel the business is established and you are getting a proper return for the investment and your labour. In the country you could find that you only have a summer season and you never exceed this figure. Even in a large village with an all-year clientele it's difficult for a B&B to exceed 50 per cent occupancy.

The year could look like this:

	In the country	In a village centre
January	0%	30%
February	0% (own holiday)	0% (own holiday)
March	10%	40%
April	15%	40%
May	20%	60%
June	50%	60%
July	95%	95%
August	95%	95%
September	50%	60%
October	15%	60%
November	5%	30%
December	5%	30%
Whole year	Average = 30%	Average = 50%

So there is a huge amount of unused capacity and your ingenuity in filling it will make a big difference to the balance sheet. If you close the usual period is from Toussaint (beginning of November) to Easter. Or just be resigned and only keep one bedroom open.

Ideas for out of season:

◆ A big reduction in price.
◆ Three nights for the price of two.
◆ Classes in all sorts of subjects.
◆ Notice on the gate saying '*ouvert*'.
◆ A big pitch for Christmas and New Year.
◆ Free champagne for a birthday.

BOOKING (*see Fig. 23*)

You must have a **foolproof** reservation calendar. If you double book, the customer will, quite rightly, make one hell of a fuss.

A good word to say about the British is that they are the best in the world for booking early. You may get the first firm booking for the following season as early as October, but the prime month is January. Next come most other nationalities who reckon that around Easter is time enough. Last are the French – after Easter and right into June still looking to book up the family holiday. I'm told it is tempting fate to book too early; after all, the worst might happen. However, there is a worldwide tendency to book later and later.

After a couple of years, and if you keep a check on the numbers, you will know by the end of March how the season is going to compare with last year.

No deposit received = no firm booking. **Be absolutely firm** about this, even with people you know well. If you are asked to hold a provisional reservation, say firmly it's only for 2 weeks. If you allow people to dither, it can mean losing an alternative good booking.

Gîtes de France recommend asking for a deposit of 25 per cent, but 15 or 20 per cent or a fixed amount are more usual. When people send the wrong

Chambres d'Hôtes BonTemps

****
****

FORMULAIRE DE RESERVATION
BOOKING FORM

Nous vous proposons de nous communiquer votre réservation par téléphone ou par e-mail immédiatement; nous la garderons 15 jours sous réserve de réception de votre acompte.
We suggest you phone or e-mail your reservation immediately and it will be held for 14 days pending arrival of your deposit.

Nom ....
Name

Adresse ....
Addresse

Tél .... E-mail ....

Date d'arrivée .... No. de nuits ....
Date of arrival   *No. of nights*

No. de personnes .... Ages si moins de 18 ans ....
No. of people   *Ages if under 18*

Nombre de chambres demandé: 1 pers ....
No. of rooms required   2 pers ....
                          3 pers ....

Lit pliant .... Lit pour bébé ....
Folding bed   *Cot*

Pension   OUI/NON   Demi-pension   OUI/NON
           yes/no   *yes/no*

Si vous n'êtes pas en pension ou demi-pension, voulez vous le dîner le premier soir ? OUI/NON
If not pension or demi-pension, would you like dinner on your first night?   *yes/no*

Montant de l'acompte ci-joint ....
Amount of deposit enclosed

Vos autres commentaires ....
Any other comments

                ....

Signature .... Date ....

Figure 23   Booking form

amount, don't be pedantic about getting it right: the object is the firm commitment. At least it does mean there is a little money coming in during the first 3 months of the year. In particular, don't let a large group mess you about: the larger the group, the more possibilities for a problem (*see Fig. 24 for a model booking receipt*).

Chambres d'Hôtes BonTemps

```
****************************
*********************
```

Date

Received from ....

Address ....

The Sum of │ £ .... │ ....

Reservation for ....

....

....

Your hosts, John and Jane, have an extensive knowledge of the area and will be pleased to help plan your visits to places of interest.

Signed

Figure 24   A receipt form

We tried to get a credit card facility from our bank, but the charge was much too high for our little business. This needs solving because we could only accept French and British cheques. Even cheques from other euroland countries attract a charge. And I understand that cheques may be withdrawn altogether soon. So for bookings from all other countries you've either got to insist on a bank transfer and accept the fee, or forgo the deposit if it's only a small amount. In the latter case we fortunately never came unstuck. Send receipts promptly, either using a bought pad or produce your own.

Be very careful on dates because the French reckon them differently. You will already know that our fortnight (14 nights) is their *quinzaine* (15 days). Similarly our 7-day-week is their *huitaine* (8 days).
Therefore:
   English booking for 4 days = 4 nights
   French booking for 4 days = 3 nights

CANCELLATIONS

Cancellations are a great bugbear, not that there's anything to be done about them. You just hope for another booking to emerge. So it might, but it was never as good: either less people or fewer nights. People not showing up and forgetting to let you know are even worse. Of course it will be those who have made a last-minute reservation with no time to send the deposit. It didn't happen often and I'm afraid it was mostly the French. Well, it is their country and they know they can easily find somewhere else. It is counter productive to say that the room will only be held until 6pm; there is practically no chance of getting anyone else at that late hour. It's even more infuriating if they have booked dinner. A proprietor told me the only time in 15 years he ever lost his temper in front of customers was just such an occasion.

PAYING

After the deposit, the remainder can be paid:

1. In full in advance. This would have to be stipulated on the booking form. Only possible with an entirely foreign clientele and if casual arrivals are not accepted. The French **will not** pay in advance; you lose custom if you try.

2. On arrival. In the flurry of a warm greeting it does come across as a bit mercenary. So only ask this of those who have not paid a deposit.

3. During the stay. If you don't accept cards they have to pay in cash. They may ask for a bill in advance in order to withdraw money from a cash point.

4. On leaving. Administratively this is much the simplest because the bill can include all the meals and any extras. We didn't have anyone leave at 4am without paying.

Accepting sterling cheques on the last day is risky in theory because they will probably be over the £100 guarantee limit. You could ask to see their passport if you are worried, but in fact we never did have a cheque bounce.

La note

This is the equivalent of our bill. It should show your establishment's name and address (have a rubber stamp), and the customer's name and address and the date. Then it should itemise their room charges and meals and any extras, deduct any deposit paid, and show the final balance to pay. The French always use pads of squared paper (I've never found out why), or perhaps you'll have it all set up on the computer.

La facture

This is the equivalent of our invoice and you are obliged to provide it if asked. We never were, but kept a pad of forms just in case. They have to be made out to a special format, so ask your accountant what has to be included.

TELEPHONE

France Télécom is the national company but it is being challenged by others. This is your umbilical chord to the outside world. It's not just a telephone line, it should also have:

1. an answerphone
2. a fax
3. a photocopy facility
4. a link to your internet server
5. a cordless extension
6. possibly a separate payphone for the guests.

These are sophisticated machines and for a large B&B it may necessitate a second line.

In spite of email, a lot of business is still done on the telephone. Ideally it should be manned from 8am to 10pm, which is simply not possible with so few of you. But you must achieve as much coverage as possible or you will lose bookings, especially last-minute ones. A cordless extension can be carried with you wherever you go on the premises.

This extension has a further use, in that it can be handed to clients for their incoming calls, of which there will be a fair number. Even in these days of the mobile phone, we still had a payphone and it was used a lot. I'm not sure it made a profit as the machine had to be hired. Even if you have a payphone on a separate line, there is very little chance of your guests having given out the number; and anyway who is going to answer it, and in which language? (*For 'telephone' French, see Fig. 25.*)

à bientôt	see you soon	faux numero	wrong number
allô (*not* allô, allô)	hullo	horloge parlante	speaking clock
annuaire	directory	il n'est pas la	he's out
c'est à quel nom?	what name is it?	ne quittez pas	hold on
c'est écrit?	how is it spelt?	quel âge à l'enfant?	how old is the child?
c'est noté	that's noted	qui est à l'appareil?	who is speaking?
coup de téléphone	phone call	raccrocher	to hang up
coupé	cut off	rappeller	to call back
excusez moi de	excuse me for	téléphoner	to call
vous déranger	disturbing you		

Figure 25   On the telephone

When you go away it's a good idea to transfer the calls to someone else with the *transfer d'appel* (call transfer) service. It has to be applied for in writing and there is a monthly charge.

COMPUTER

I wouldn't think anyone starts in business these days without one. Maybe you're bringing it from the UK, in which case it will be already set up with English programmes and QUERTY keyboard. These items are only available in France in specialist shops, otherwise they sell the French versions. If your French is shaky, you may have difficulty with the instructions, and if you are used to an English keyboard, a different one will drive you to distraction. What's more, you'll have difficulty with a helpline without fluent French.

Although potential customers may have seen your web site and there is a booking form, they will invariably contact you by email with a question or two. I think it's mostly to check that you really exist. In fact the majority of contact with clients before they arrive is now via email. If you have some standard letters ready drafted in French and English it's quick to reply.

Tip of the day: only the 'True Type' fonts support the euro symbol.

SNAIL MAIL

Letter writing is obviously a dying art, we had one preliminary enquiry by letter in ten years. On the other hand you have sometimes got to write back as there are all sorts of matters to be sorted out, and occasionally people can't be reached any other way. (*For 'Post Office' French see Fig. 26.*) For really difficult letters in French you must pay a translation service, but if you want to do it yourself here's how (*Fig. 27*).

Boîte Postale xxx/BD xxx	PO Box xxx
carnet	book of 1st class stamps
cedex	system for very large users
code postale	post code
expéditeur/exp	from
facteur	postman
faire suivre	please forward
paquet	parcel
par avion	airmail
la poste	post office
lettre recommandé	recorded delivery
lettre recommandée avec avis de reception	recorded delivery with signed return slip
service économique	second class post
service prioritaire	first class post
surtaxe	postage due
timbre vert	2nd class stamp

The post codes consist of the department numbers (they are in alphabetical order), followed by the town number. The chief town is always '000'. Thus '01000' is the chief town in the department of 'Aine', and '01640' is a village in that department.

Figure 26   The Post Office

INSURANCE

All property in France must be insured, whether there is a mortgage or not, but you will need further public liability insurance. Cover should be for the following:

◆ The hosts, their family and animals.

◆ All the buildings and fixed equipment such as swings and sports installations.

◆ Equipment for the guests' use such as bicycles, table-tennis, badminton.

Openings and endings in decreasing order of formality

le 29 février 2004

Monsieur le Maire
Veuillez agréer, Monsieur le Maire, l'expression de mes sentiments respectueux.
Veuillez agréer, Monsieur le Maire, l'assurance de mes sentiments distinguées.
Veuillez recevoir, Monsieur le Maire, mes salutations distinguées.

Monsieur,
Je vous prie, Monsieur, d'accepter l'expression de mes sentiments les meilleurs.
Recevez, Monsieur, mes sentiments les meilleurs.

Chère Madame,
Veuillez croire, chère Madame, à l'assurance de mes sentiments distingués.
Je vous prie de croire, chère Madame, à l'expression de mes meilleurs sentiments.
Veuillez croire, chère Madame, à mes sentiments très cordiaux.
Avec mes sentiments les meilleurs.
En attendant le plaisir de faire votre connaissance.

Chère Madame Dubois,
Cordialement.

Cher Jean,
Amicalement

Figure 27   Writing letters

◆ *Table d'hôte* and the risk of food poisoning (this is obligatory).

◆ Activities organized by the proprietors away from the premises such as visits, hiking, riding and transportation to these.

◆ Swimming pool and its machinery.

◆ Potentially dangerous features such as a lake, river, mill pond.

A particular problem for B&B owners is that you cannot insure against theft by the guests without a full hotel insurance, the reason being that you have invited them in; they didn't break in. Discuss this with your insurers because it is a worry if you have any antiques. There are the same problems of under insurance as in the UK if the premiums are not increased every year. If you make a claim, do not sign that they have paid up in full until a good time afterwards, in case anything else turns up. Insurers will refuse to pay for a chimney fire if you cannot produce a certificate that it has been swept in the past 12 months.

ACCOUNTANT

The French income tax forms are complicated and are naturally written in the French version of officialese. You'll never manage it correctly by yourself. The alternative to employing an accountant is to go to the tax office during March and they will do it for you at no charge. They also have a half day's *permanence* (attendance) in every commune for that purpose.

This may suffice for the first year or two and if your affairs are straightforward, but it is much better to employ an accountant from the start. Once the business is registered at the chamber of commerce, it is **essential**. Ask all the British residents you know if they can recommend someone. It is not necessary for the accountant to be local as everything can be sent by mail or email. If it's a British national, then they can handle your foreign business as well.

There exists in France a service unknown in the UK called *Centre de Gestion des Entreprises*. It is a government organisation and their function is to help small firms. They also act as accountants and are situated in most small towns. They are very helpful but are unlikely to speak English and are not conversant with international taxation.

I'm afraid my bookkeeping only ran to a simple double entry book, totalled monthly. Then I had to submit all the bills stapled together, month by month, and copies of the bank account were obtained direct. This is not very sophisticated and your accountant may demand more or recommend a suitable computer programme. One good thing is the books are done in February, well out of season.

For a substantial business run from your own home you will be able to claim 80 per cent of electricity, water, gas, telephone and *Taxe Foncière* as business expenses, plus 50 per cent for the car. I would argue that the 80 per cent for the telephone should be increased now. The utility bills are paid by direct debit, but this can lead to the complacency of not scrutinising them closely before they are paid and you could miss a nasty surprise somewhere. *For a general administration glossary, see Fig. 28.*

annulation (f)	cancellation	quinzaine (f)	fortnight
annuler	to cancel	reçu (m)	receipt
arrhes (f)	deposit	répondeur (m)	answerphone
assurance (f)	insurance	réservation (f)	reservation
bénéfice (m)	profit	saison (f)	season
calendrier (m)	calendar	bas saison	low season
congé (m)	leave	haute saison	high season
complet	full	hors saison	out of season
comptable (m)	accountant	sans fil (m)	cordless (phone)
disponible	available	séjour (m)	stay
hébergement (m)	lodging	semaine (f)	week
huitaine (f)	week	subvention (f)	grant
jour (m)	day	tarif (m)	tariff
jour férié	public holiday	télécopie, fax (m)	fax
ordinateur (m)	computer	téléphone (m)	phone
pension	full board	vacance (f)	holiday
demi-pension	half board	vacances scolaires	school holiday
perte (f)	loss	week-end (m)	week-end
portable (m)	mobile phone		

Figure 28   Glossary

TIPS TO MAKE IT PAY

◆ Only borrow the amount you are sure you can afford.

◆ Investigate grants.

◆ Accept sterling cheques.

◆ Except for last minute bookings, do not accept reservations without a deposit.

◆ Make a target of 30 per cent occupancy for the year.

TIP TO IMPROVE YOUR FRENCH

◆ Buy a dictating machine for less than £20 and listen to yourself reading French.

9

Keep it Clean

CLEANING

I hope you like housework because there will be a lot of it. I once saw a B&B advertised as being 'clean'. Cheeky. Was it to imply that most B&Bs are not? Of course you have got to be and, I admit, cleaner than most of us are in our own homes, since there is no leeway for anything otherwise in a commercial premises. 'There's a hair in the shower and it's not mine' says Mrs Guest. Not in our establishment, thankfully, though lapses do occur and you will be covered with shame. There's nothing for it but to apologise and attend to the problem straight away. Bedrooms and bathrooms need a quick clean every day (10 minutes) and a thorough clean for new guests. Hotels allow 20 minutes for changeovers; I doubt if we achieved that. The family room for 4 took an hour if there was a cot or folding bed to be put up or dismantled.

Sometimes guests made their own beds, which was nice, but if asked I always insisted we would do it. Make the beds very neatly with hospital corners. The public rooms need cleaning every day. You have to **insist** that people vacate their room by 10am or you'll never get done by lunch time. If the cleaning runs into the afternoon, the guests could arrive, and the rooms may not be ready. It happened once. I sat them down with a cup of tea, and had to think fast for a good excuse. Some B&Bs stipulate that guests must not arrive before 4pm. We found that 2pm was alright because few actually came at that time; most arrived between 4 and 6pm.

MAINTENANCE

Everything broken or damaged must be seen to **immediately**. A German guest complained bitterly about the French on this matter and said it was the reason he'd chosen a proprietor with an English sounding name from the holiday guide. So keep the reputation up to teutonic standards! Admittedly, keeping all those bathrooms functioning gave us more grief than all the other rooms put together; we seemed to need a resident plumber. With careless use something was always going wrong. It helps to keep spares of as many items as possible.

Even if there aren't many guests in the winter, or even if you close, there's little respite. Make a list of 'Things To Do This Winter'. It should include all the regular maintenance, the shopping to upgrade the rooms, the 'spring' cleaning, and the redecorating. It will be quite a list, and you won't get through it, but do try.

LINEN

You probably never gave it much thought before. From now on it will loom large in your consciousness. If the good news is that French bed sizes are the same as UK, the bad news is that their linen is quite different. You will probably bring what you already have, but it will not be enough and sooner or later it needs replacing. The big supermarkets have 'white sales' in January and February which are good for curtains, bedspreads, pillows, duvets – all things where matching replacements won't be wanted. The mail order catalogues also have good special offers at that time.

Linen
   Wash under-blankets & machine washable bedspreads
   Dry-clean bedspreads, duvets, curtains, & blankets on a 2- or 3-year rotation
   Turn out linen and cleaning cupboard and clean
   Most pillows with man-made fillings can be washed, or at least wash the covers
   Check all linen for mending

Bathrooms & WCs
   De-scale chrome fittings and shower heads
   Clean wall tiling & shower cubicles
   Scrub tiled floors
   Freshen up tiled joints with joint whitener
   Wash shower curtains
   Check any gas heaters well before the first guest arrives

Bedrooms & Corridors
   Brush ceilings and plastered walls with cobweb brush
   Vacuum textured walls such as stone, brick or crepi
   Move all furniture and clean behind
   Vacuum inside wardrobes and drawers
   Turn mattress at the very least once a year and vacuum both sides
   Treat stains on rugs & carpets
   Clean mirrors & difficult-to-reach windows
   Clean light fittings
   Check coat hangers & room keys

Public Rooms
   Clean walls, ceilings, windows, lights, and move furniture as for bedrooms
   Wash removable upholstery covers or clean with proprietary product
   Turn out store cupboards & clean
   Throw away old tourist literature
   Dry-clean curtains every year if there is an open fire or smoking is permitted
   Have fire extinguisher verified & check that smoke detectors function
   Check games for missing pieces; tidy library
   Remove indoor plants to somewhere warmer if room is not heated
   Have chimney swept

Kitchen
   Brush walls & ceiling with cobweb brush
   Wash light shades & fluorescent covers
   Scrub wall tiling
   Turn out larder & throw away old stock
   Check home made preserves left over from last year
   Defrost freezer & put on one side products nearing expiry date and leftovers for using up
      yourselves
   Clean cooker, fridge, dishwasher, washing machine
   Wash all furniture & fittings
   Renew cooker hood filter
   Scrub floor
   Have boiler serviced & fire extinguisher verified
   Update recipe file
   De-scale appliances & check cups & teapots for staining

Figure 29   Aide memoire for winter maintenance and cleaning

Sheets

The French have stayed with cotton more than the UK. There's no doubt that it is best and good hotels all over the world have cotton. It should be good quality or it will feel like being in hospital. Quality is defined by the number of threads to the inch: standard is 180, the best is 300. However, a B&B is not the Ritz and poly-cotton is so much easier to wash, to dry, and to iron. If you have coloured or patterned sheets, the colours will fade with all that washing so you'll never be able to mix in any more, even if available. That's why most people stay with white. The quantity needed varies with the length of stay and how often they are changed, certainly twice a week for grade 4. At boarding school we had clean sheets once a fortnight, but times are different now. Start with 3 sets per bed and see how you get on.

Pillows

A decision to be made before leaving the UK is whether to stay with our rectangular pillows, or to have the French 60x60cm size. Neither the rectangular pillows nor the pillow cases are available in France. It's normal to give 2 pillows each, but note that the square ones are usually paired with a bolster. Most of the rest of the world doesn't like bolsters. A few guests will bring their own, which reveals their low opinion of what they expect to be provided. In any case have some spares as older people will often ask for a third one, and a feather pillow is sometimes requested.

Under blankets

These are always necessary and they **must** be waterproof on single and folding beds where you expect children. You can have waterproof on adults beds too; after all, small children often get in with their parents, though some people may object. They should be washed frequently so you need some spares.

Duvets and blankets

Again a difference: the British have nearly all changed to duvets. The French not so much. When duvets are used they are accompanied by an ordinary set of sheets along with the duvet and its cover. For a B&B this is a very good idea because washing a duvet cover and a bottom sheet with integral valance is a chore after only one night. But duvets are really too hot in France in the summer so you need some blankets as well, and therefore could consider having blankets only.

Bedspreads

Blankets need a bedspread. Be bold and have something brightly patterned because they are such a dominant feature of the room. You will need a lightweight one for the summer, and a warmer one for the winter. If the winter one is quilted for warmth, this reduces the weight of blankets.

Towels

Yes, lots. It's normal to give a large and a small one per person. The Dutch like clean towels every day. The recommendation is twice a week for grade 3, and every day, if used, for grade 4. The problem when not changing towels that day is how to get them dry in the greater part of the year when the bathroom isn't heated. The guests will drape them all over the place, even out of the window. Tut, tut, we don't want to look like a shanty town. If they were very wet, I would put them on the line. There should be a matching washable bath mat. Towels are a problem with a swimming pool. Most guests bring their own swimming towels, but you could find your best ones taken outside. Offering swimming towels, gratis, helps.

Table cloths, napkins and serviettes

Cloths rarely last for more than one meal, or you could have mats for dinner. Paper serviettes are alright for breakfast, but for dinner you should have fabric. It's all yet more washing.

LAUNDRY

It would have been good to have had a big commercial washing machine. But they cost so much that two domestic ones are better value, then the visitors can also use one. In fact I beat the living daylights out of one domestic machine. There was a **lot** of washing and it needed doing **every day** in the season. The machine needs to have minimum wash programmes because a lot of the washing is after only one night. You can just about manage without a dryer in the south, but it is the best way of keeping the towels fluffy. Dryer, or not, you need plenty of washing-line because the guests often wash their smalls or hang up their swimming things. An ironing machine is not a luxury in this situation – not a commercial one, just a domestic flat bed type will make all the difference. You will miss the UK airing cupboard, but really the climate is so much drier that it's not necessary.

If all the laundry is getting on top of you, how about sending it out? If one person is trying to run a B&B on their own, it is the one big time saver that could make the difference between success and utter exhaustion. A laundry will also hire out linen. To find one look in your local shops to see who is an agent for a dry cleaners; that firm will also probably do laundry.

EQUIPMENT

Keeping all the machines in working order made for plenty of repair bills. Put the guarantees in a safe place, you'll need them. (For list of equipment see Fig. 30, for glossary of housekeeping terms see Fig. 31.)

THE KITCHEN

You have got to be **very careful** in the kitchen:

1. Wash your hands.
2. Don't allow pets in the kitchen.
3. Separate chopping board for meat.
4. Check temperatures of fridge and freezer.
5. And have everything super clean.

Cooking in quantity makes for a lot of fat going down the sink and it'll surely block one day. One of my favourite French words is *catastrophe*, which describes this situation. There is a nifty gadget called a *furet* (ferret) which is basically a screw on the end of a long flexible rod, with a handle to turn it: obtainable from ironmongers it works a treat. Another way is to put *soude caustique* (caustic soda) down the sink. It's toxic stuff but is obtainable from supermarkets. A septic tank needs re-activating afterwards.

CURTAINS

Until recently French homes seldom had curtains; the shutters served the same function. You do need them now for an international clientele.

For Starting Up

Refrigerator	Computer
Dishwasher	Telephone, fax, answer phone
Washing machine	Electric drill
Domestic cooker	Sewing machine
Large chest freezer	Iron and ironing board
Large kettle and coffee machine	Trailer or small van
Vacuum cleaner	Ride-on mower ⎫
Large microwave	Strimmer ⎬ if large garden
Kitchen robot	

Later

2nd vacuum cleaner (1 upstairs, 1 downstairs)
Large larder-type fridge (keep original one for visitors)
Ironing machine
2nd iron and ironing board (for visitors)
Car battery charger (for self and visitors)
Replace cooker with large commercial type with hood
2nd kettle, 2nd coffee machine
Drying machine
2nd washing machine (for self and visitors)
Electric oil filled radiator ⎫
Electric fan heater ⎬ for standby use
Bottle gas heater ⎭
Hired payphone (for visitors)
Safe
2 men's, 2 women's bicycles (children's optional)
Gas barbecue
Electric log-cutting machine (if log fire)
Electric garden shredder ⎫
Chain saw ⎬ if large garden
Electric hedge cutter ⎭

Figure 30   The equipment you will need

However, the inward-opening windows make for problems. If the curtains are close to the window you can't have the window open and the curtains closed at the same time. So do try and set the curtains back from the window. Then explain to foreign clients that the shutters really work and in hot weather they should open the windows and latch the shutters only partly shut. Curtains have become more elaborate than they used to be, and expensive. If you have tie-backs it will be you who is tying them back prettily every day; it's all extra minutes when doing the rooms. If the window is overlooked, you'll need net curtains as well, mounted on the frame itself because of the inward opening.

SMOKING

You need a policy:

- No restrictions. Have plenty of ash trays about, including in the bedrooms and on the dinner table.

- No smoking in certain rooms, say dining-room and possibly lounge. Have notices in these rooms and ash trays in the bedrooms. Or one bedroom could be specifically designated as being non-smoking.

- Totally non-smoking premises. Needs to be stated in all advertisements and your brochure, plus notices in all the rooms. Difficult to apply if you accept one-night stays. It is illegal not to accept smokers at all, so the best you could do is restrict them to out of doors.

THE WILDLIFE

Most of us Brits are townies and are quite unprepared for this aspect of living in the country. By wildlife, I mean the ones with none, two, four, six, or eight legs: flying, scampering, crawling or slithering indoors. There are so many more of them than we are used to, and keeping them at bay was a constant battle. The trouble is the guests don't understand this. One of the bedrooms was invaded by flying ants. 'No problem,' we say 'we'll spray it while you're having dinner.' 'Oh no,' they say, 'we don't approve of chemicals; we keep a health food shop.' Of course.

In the country rodents are a particular problem. There are many more of them even than in British rural areas. However many cats there are, they won't make an impression on the numbers. At the first evidence of a mouse, clear the drawer or shelf and set a trap. When one is caught, keep setting the trap for a couple of days to see if there is a family. I prefer this to poison because we did have cats. There were a few rats outside, but also another rodent peculiar to the south called a *loir*. In size it's between a mouse and a rat but it has a hairy tail. They eat fruit and seeds, so they don't come into the body of the house, but they love roof spaces and guests can complain about the noise. Get the kind of trap from the ironmonger's that catches them alive and then release the creatures in a wood. For a swarm of bees, try and find a bee keeper because they are a protected species. If a nest can't be reached and for wasps and hornets call the fire brigade. There will be a charge. For other insects you need to have ready an arsenal of repellents. Use a spray at the first sight of a column of marching ants. The guests may complain about mosquitoes; we kept a supply of appropriate products.

THE WELCOME

First impressions are important, especially the room temperature. In very hot weather it looks thoughtful to have the shutters partially closed to keep the sun out. In cold weather of course the bedroom and bathroom should be warm. Everyone loves freebies. Usually it's a small soap, sachet of shampoo/shower gel, and a box of tissues; all obtainable from the 'cash and

abat-jour (m)	lamp shade	nappe (f)	table cloth
alèse (f)	under blanket	nettoyer	to clean
araignée (f)	spider	oreiller (m)	pillow
toile d'araignée (f)	spider's web	taie d'oreiller (f)	pillow case
aspirateur (m)	vacuum cleaner	panier (m)	linen basket
bac à graisse (m)	grease trap	(en) panne	broken
balai (m)	broom	pièce détachée (f)	spare part
balayer	to sweep	pince à linge (f)	clothes peg
cendrier (m)	ash tray	pipi (m)	wee-wee
cintre (m)	coat hanger	poignée (f)	handle
clé (f)	key	porte savon (f)	soap dish
corde à linge (f)	clothes line	poussière (f)	dust
couette (f)	duvet, quilt	propre	clean
housse de couette (f)	duvet cover	ramoner	to sweep a chimney
couverture (f)	blanket	repasser	to iron
crochet (m)	hook	fer à repasser (m)	iron
débarrasser	to clear away	planchèa repasser (f)	ironing board
déshumidficateur (m)	dehumidifier	rideau (m)	curtain
drap (m)	sheet	sale	dirty
drap housse	fitted sheet	savon (m)	soap
drap plat	flat sheet	savonette (f)	small soap
eau de javel (f)	bleach	serpillière (f)	floor cloth
fourmi (f)	ant	serrure (f)	lock
gant (m)	face flannel	serviette (f)	towel, serviette
jeté de lit (m)	bedspread	shampooing (m)	shampoo
lampe (f)	(electric) bulb	tapis de bain (m)	bath mat
lessive (f)	washing powder	torchon (m)	dishcloth
linge de lit (m)	bed linen	traversin (m)	bolster
(en) marche	working	taie de traversin	bolster case
moustique (m)	mosquito	tringle (f)	curtain rod

Figure 31 Glossary

carry'. Hotel suppliers have a better quality range but the minimum order is about 500 and there is a hefty delivery charge for 'small' orders. It is best to have individual sachets of these items: people don't like using soaps and bottles that have previously been used by someone else. At grade 4, expectations are high and you should provide good quality products, renewed frequently, together with fresh flowers and a bowl of fresh fruit. In most *départements* there should be a free guide to what's on, published either by a local newspaper or the tourist office, and it's a good idea to put one in each room.

TIPS FOR MAKING IT PAY

- Have only white linen.
- Buy mostly in the January sales.
- Have table mats or non-iron tablecloths.

TIP FOR IMPROVING YOUR FRENCH

- Buy a disc of French songs. You should be able to find Edith Piaf or Jaques Brel.

10

Dealing with Officialdom

On setting up a business in France you will come across their immense bureaucracy. With the added disadvantage of another language, you may find it daunting. However, you must try and understand it because the costs are high and ignorance can lead to paying more than necessary. Although rates and income tax are lower, the high social security payments bring the total to more than the UK. Unfortunately, most taxes and final metered charges for utilities have to be paid in the 6 months from October to March, which is just when a B&B is receiving least income. There are severe penalties for late payment. Most of you will have been in salaried employment in the UK where all taxes, excepting rates, are paid by the employer. As a self-employed person in France, you will be taken aback by the number of tax demands that keep arriving in the letter-box. The information in this chapter must be considered as only a precis of the situation.

One could wish that the multitude of rules and regulations to which we are subjected should be available in writing in plain French. They are not, and if you ask for information at the tax or social security office, you are likely to get an evasive answer and it will differ between departments. The reason is that jurisprudence, i.e. previous court decisions on the matter, are only binding on the case in hand and not universally. So any official is still free to make their own interpretations.

It doesn't help that neither *chambres d'hôtes* nor *table d'hôte* have a legal definition, therefore officials do vary as to which business category you belong to. Sometimes they will allow you to be a *gîte*, in which case you are just letting part of your own home. But particularly if you have a *table d'hôte*, they will say you are a fully-fledged business, which is quite a different matter. It really depends on the scale of the enterprise.

You will find the French language is choc-a-block of acronyms: *CPAM, URSSAF, SAMU, SMIC*, to name only a few. I know they exist in English too, but I don't think there are quite so many.

PART 1 – BEFORE THE BUSINESS IS REGISTERED

IDENTITY CARD *(Carte de Séjour)*

Non EU nationals will need a visa before they come, and remember there's been a lot of hassle over illegal immigrants lately. EU nationals should apply at the town hall for a *Carte de Séjour* within 3 months of arrival. It can take months, but is a useful proof of identity in many situations.

FAMILY BOOK *(Livret de Famille)*

In France this replaces birth, marriage, adoption and death certificates. You will sometimes be asked for it and will have to produce the relevant British certificates instead. So make sure you possess all yours and your children's before leaving the UK.

BANK ACCOUNT *(Compte en Banque)*

Sterling account

I am sure you will want to keep a sterling account. Shop around for one with the least transfer charges to France, because there are large differences.

French account

You will have a non-interest-bearing cheque account with a monthly statement as in the UK. It is a criminal offence to allow a cheque to bounce, known as a *cheque en bois*, literally 'a wooden cheque'. In view of this, bank cheque cards are not necessary. However, you will often be asked for identification. This will be the *Carte de Séjour*, but if you don't have one, you will have to carry your passport. Paying by direct debit card (*le plastique*) in now widespread, and there are plenty of cash withdrawal machines. Note that cheques cannot be stopped without a limited number of official reasons, and changing your mind is not one of them. Although interest rates are now minimal, it's still worth having another savings account.

RATES 1

Taxe Foncière

Payable in full by 15th October. The *Taxe Foncière* is based on the letting value of the land, whether built on or not. It must be paid by the owner of the land. If you buy mid-year it will be apportioned between the two owners by the *notaire*. Both of these rates 1 and 2 add up to much less than rates in the UK.

RATES 2

Taxe d'Habitation

Payable in full by 15th November. It is levied on the resident occupier of the property on January 1st each year. This is tough on the person who moves out on 2nd January but nice for the one who moves in. If the property is not furnished on 1st January, no one has to pay. There are some exemptions or reductions for retired or handicapped people. It is calculated on the size of the buildings and the land.

INCOME TAX *(Impôt sur le Revenu)*

For most income arising in the UK, you can elect for it to be taxed either in the UK or France, and there is a double taxation agreement between the two countries so that tax is not paid twice.

Income tax **must** be paid in France if you **or** your spouse and children stay in the country for more than 183 days (ignoring days of arrival and departure). If you are switching between countries for the first year or two and the B&B is not operating yet, it might be worth arranging your visits such that you don't involve the French taxman. You must register your presence in France at the local *Centre des Impôts*, then you will automatically be sent a tax return form in February to be returned by 24th March.

You will hear in due course:

1. Nothing to pay. Guard this statement because it has beneficial uses.

2. For small amounts and in the first year the tax must be paid in full by 15th September.

3. Tax can be paid in 3 instalments known as *tiers provisionnels*. They will be due on the 15th of February, May and September. The first 2 are estimated and the last is the actual sum. This is for those who know how to invest their money instead of giving it to the tax man.

4. *Paiement mensuel* (monthly payment). You pay an estimated sum by direct debit for the first 10 months and only pay the last 2 months if there is a shortfall. It is due on the 8th of the month. This is for those who can't set aside money for their taxes and need a monthly system.

Personal and children's allowances are fairly similar to the UK but you can include elderly relatives as dependants. The fiscal year runs from January 1st, and tax is due on the previous year's income not the current year as in the UK.

HEALTH INSURANCE *(Caisse Primaire d'Assurance Maladie/CPAM)*

The E111 form (obtainable from UK post offices) entitles EU residents to refunds for health care in France on the same basis as the French. It lasts for a stay of up to 1 year. If you make a claim, keep a record of the *No. de Sécurité Sociale* printed at the top of the statement you will receive, then you can use this number in future without bothering about the UK form. You will have to pay in full, then, to make a claim, send the form you will have received to the *CPAM* office in your *chef-lieu* (county town). The refund cheque will be sent either to your home, or will be paid direct into a French bank if you have enclosed the slip (*bancaire*) found in every cheque book.

At the end of the year you **must** register either with *CPAM* or a *mutuelle* (private health scheme) and you will have to declare this to obtain the *Carte de Séjour*. Depending on the type of scheme chosen, they may refund the full 100% of all medical costs; ask at *CPAM* for the list of firms.

Retired EU residents can transfer their own country's health rights to France. There are no contributions to pay and you will receive all the same benefits as the French. For information write to the Department of Social Security (address in the Appendix). Note that the health services are not free to retired people as they are in the UK. Hospital is generally free (except for a lodging fee), but otherwise the state pays 35% to 70% unless you have a *maladie longue durée* (long term chronic illness) in which case you can apply for 100% reimbursement.

You do not register with a doctor or dentist in the British way; it's a totally free choice. As long as they are *conventioné* (affiliated to the social security) then the charges are regulated, otherwise they can charge more and you will not get a full refund.

PENSION

Probably there's a gap between leaving employment in the UK and registering your business in France. Possibly it's several years and you are not paying into a pension scheme anywhere. You could regret this when the time comes, and you should consider paying voluntary contributions until starting on a French scheme. For information contact the Inland Revenue National Insurance Contributions Office, (address in the Appendix). If you already draw the UK state or other government pension, it can be sent direct to your French bank in euros at a good exchange rate.

SOCIAL SECURITY CONTRIBUTION *(Contributions Sociales)*

Payable by 15th December. Just a little contribution to the government because their social security has run out of money. Based on your income.

DRINKS LICENCE *(Licence Débit de Boissons)*

All *chambres d'hôtes* **must** have a licence, even if only serving breakfasts. The licences are in 4 categories and cover the sale of beverages and alcoholic drinks. For breakfasts only you need a Category 1 Licence (*Licence de Boissons Sans Alcool*), which allows the sale of all non-alcoholic beverages.

A *table d'hôte* needs a Category 2 Licence (*Petite Licence Restaurant*). This allows you to serve all beverages in Category 1 plus Category 2 which includes non-distilled drinks such as wine, beer, champagne and cider.

Ask at the town hall where to obtain these licences; it will probably be a *tabac*. It's a simple matter of giving your name and address; there is no fee and they last permanently. Both of these licences **only** allow beverages and drinks to be consumed on the premises and they **must not** be charged extra. In addition the alcoholic drinks **must** accompany a meal.

If you want to keep a wine cellar and charge for the drinks, then you will need a Category 3 or 4 licence. These are expensive, involve much negotiation with officialdom and also have tax implications.

MOTOR VEHICLES

EU driving licences are valid in France, but if you have an accident, there can be problems, so it is better to change to a French *permis de conduire* (driving licence). This is only possible after you have a *Carte de Séjour*. Other nationalities have to take lessons and a test. On buying a car you will be issued with a *Carte Grise* (log book) which, together with the insurance and driving licence, should be carried at all times in the car. There is a severe points system for offences, and in the extreme you could lose your licence. This would be a serious drawback for the business, but there is a jokey little car called a *véhicule sans permis* that can be driven without a licence. All vehicles over 4 years old must have a *Contrôle Tecnique* (MOT) every 2 years. Insurance and no claims bonuses are similar to the UK but more expensive because of their high accident rate and the amount of car theft. The vehicle tax has been abolished.

TV LICENCE *(Service de la Redevance de l'Audiovisuel)*

When a TV is bought in France, the shop will notify the licensing authority and a demand is sent automatically. It must be paid even if you only receive British programmes via satellite. Pensioners on a low income are exempt, but must apply to the address on the demand. If there are TVs in all the bedrooms, there is a licence fee for sets in excess of 3, but it is reduced by 30%.

THE POLICE *(Les Gendarmes)*

We found them courteous and helpful and they found our car within 3 days of it being stolen. Then the insurance company paid for a first class train ticket to go and collect it. Then when we went to the wrong police station a police driver took us to the correct one. And one thing more: the parents of one of the *gendarmes* came and stayed for a week in our *chambres d'hôtes*. Go along and make yourself known because it just could happen that you get some troublesome guests and need their presence.

FIRE AND AMBULANCE *(Sapeurs Pompiers)*

Fortunately I haven't had first-hand knowledge of these services but I'm told they are good. Unlike the UK, the emergency ambulances in the country are red and are run by the fire service. In a small town it is voluntary and the members will include one of the local doctors. The non-emergency ambulances are run quite separately by private companies.

PART 2 – AFTER THE BUSINESS IS REGISTERED

CHAMBER OF COMMERCE *(Chambre de Commerce)*

This is not a club as in the UK; it is a government office. In France you cannot just open up for business, it **has to be registered** with the *chambre* designated for that trade. For a B&B it is the *Chambre de Commerce*. It will be situated in your *chef-lieu* (county town). The point at which you have to register the business is a very grey area, and even *Gîtes de France* will not give definitive guidance. It depends on whether the B&B income is your main income. When it reaches this point you **should** register.

However, you will want to delay registering for as long as possible because it brings with it all the **obligatory** social security, health and pension payments. The registration applies exclusively to the one type of business named and any ancillary activities. For a B&B you are allowed, for example, to charge guests for hiring bicycles and doing laundry. There is a fee for registration, but no further annual payments.

You will be given a '*SIRET*' number to identify the business, and a '*SIREN*' number which identifies your *TVA* status. This *SIREN* number with FR added to the end can be used when buying goods (usually wholesale) in the UK without paying VAT, but mostly it's too much palaver.

BANK ACCOUNT *(Compte en Banque)*

French bank

It is **essential** to have a separate account for the business. Don't put any transactions through this account that shouldn't be there or you could have the tax inspector asking for details.

Sterling account

You are sure to receive some sterling cheques and will send them to your British (or Isle of Man or Channel Islands) bank. Either you must have a separate business account, or all sterling cheques will have to be treated as cash transactions.

HEALTH INSURANCE *(Mutuelle)*

Once the business is registered, joining a *Mutuelle* is **compulsory** for the person named. This a private company approved to administer health insurance. You will automatically be sent a list of names to choose from. They administer all claims and refunds and you pay according to income, but there are reductions for the first 2 years. Payment is twice a year. You have to pay even if you are over the retirement age of 60. You will be issued with a *Carte Vitale* (plastic card) which contains your details. You have to pay the medical fees in full, but presentation of the card makes the refund automatic without any further action on your part. A few medics are not in the scheme; then you have to make a claim on the form provided.

PENSION *(Assurance Vieillesse)*)

Again, once the business is registered, joining a pension scheme is **obligatory** for the person named. In this there is no choice of names. For the self-employed *commerçant* (tradesman) it has to be *Organic*. Unless you already have a working lifetime's contributions, you have to pay, even if over retirement age. Since the money paid in is not taxed, and as it will come back one day, it is good value. If one of the marriage partners does not have any other pension arrangement, it should be possible to join the same scheme as a *conjoint collaborateur*. Ask for details.

VAT *(Taxe sur la Valeur Ajoutée/TVA)*

Registering with the *Chambre de Commerce* means that you may be subject to *TVA*. The criteria is that bed and breakfast alone is considered *non professionnel* because the business mainly consists of letting furnished rooms. Once a *table d'hôte* is added, the business becomes *professionnel* because you are selling services and if the profit is more than ½ of your total income you may be subjected to *TVA*. Your accountant will advise you.

The French government makes 40% of its income from *TVA*. It's cheap to collect too, because you will be doing most of the work.

TVA has to be paid 5 times a year, 4 times estimated and a 5th on the actual figure. The amount due is the difference between the amount of *TVA* paid to other people, subtracted from the amount you have charged your customers. This has nothing to do with the profitability of the business and has to be paid even when making a loss. However, in the first year there could be a refund as you can claim for capital expenditure in the years before registration. The rates that mainly affect a B&B are:

   5.5% on food, hotel rooms, water bills
   19.6% on everything else

Since a *chambres d'hôtes* price comprises both room and breakfast, it is taken as being 75% for the room with *TVA* at 5.5%, and 25% for the breakfast with *TVA* at 19.6%. Even if your guest does not have breakfast, it is still assessed this way. The French government has petitioned Brussels to be allowed to reduce the 19.6% *TVA* on restaurant meals, so this may change.

Don't be too frightened about the amount of money you may have to pay. It's not all that much because in a B&B you will be claiming a lot back – the outgoings are high. The real problem with it is the amount of time it takes. There is no set amount that a small business can opt to pay, as there is in the UK. To claim back the *TVA* paid out, it has to be justified, and this means getting a *facture* (invoice) for **every** purchase. A *facture* **has** to show the amounts with, and without *TVA*, plus the registered number of the originator. A B&B is such a capital intensive venture that it could just pay to register voluntarily, before you have to. The situation must be discussed with your accountant.

SOCIAL SECURITY *(Union de Recourvrement de Sécurite Social et des Allocations Familiales (URSSAF))*

This is the main social security payment and is additional to health and retirement schemes. It is based on income and there is an exoneration for incomes below €4,018. It can be paid monthly on the 20th by direct debit, or quarterly on the 15th of May, August, November and February.

BUSINESS RATES *(Taxe Professionnelle)*

When part of a domestic property is set aside for business use, such as a B&B, then there is an additional tax to pay. It is based on the area and is payable by 15th December.

THE BLACK *(Le Noir, Le Black)*

It is rife in France, but **don't have anything to do with it.** It's not your country, and it's not your problem. You wouldn't be able to declare any payments as business expenses.

Furthermore the penalties are:

◆ €30,000 fine and 2 years in prison.

◆ If a person working for you has an accident at work, the social security will investigate.

◆ The income tax inspectors will asses the persons concerned for back taxes.

WHERE TO GET HELP IN FRANCE

You don't need to think the French themselves get it right all the time either. So you'll not be alone. Don't worry or spend any sleepless nights. Just do it, or pay it, and see what happens. Probably nothing.

However, if things have really gone wrong and you do need help, contact the following:

◆ *Mairie* (town hall) for everything local.

◆ *Office de Tourisme/Syndicat d'Initiative* for everything to do with tourism.

◆ *Caisse Primaire d'Assurance Maladie/CPAM* in chief town for the state health insurance.

◆ *Trésor Public* in nearest town for taxes.

◆ *France Télécom* for telephone service.

◆ Electricity/gas/water see *Yellow Pages*.

◆ The British Embassy in Paris will give you the name of the nearest British consulate for citizenship problems, (address in Appendix).

If you have a problem, it's best to go and talk direct to the official concerned, preferably with a French person to help you. If appropriate, present your plausible excuses (not that you didn't understand because you're foreign). They have more discretion than their British counterparts and you might at the very least get let off a penalty.

TIPS FOR MAKING IT PAY

◆ Check all demands for money, including official ones, to see you aren't paying too much.

banque (f)	bank	noir (m)	the black
chèque (m)	cheque	pénalité (f)	penalty
chèque en bois	bounced cheque	relevé bancaire RIB (m)	bank identity slip
chéquier (m)	cheque-book	relevé bancaire de compte	bank statement
chiffre d'affaires (m)	turnover	mensuel	monthly
commerçant (m)	tradesman	taxe (f)	tax
compte (m)	account	hors taxe/HT	without VAT
dégrèvement (m)	reduction	tiers paiement (m)	quarterly
entreprise (f)	business	travailleur independant (m)	self employed
fonctionnaire (m)	official	toutes taxes comprises/TTC	including VAT
imprimé (m)	form	TVA (f)	VAT

Figure 32 Glossary

- ◆ Pay by the due dates to avoid penalties.
- ◆ Ask shops you regularly visit for an account.
- ◆ Go and see the official concerned if you have any queries.

TIP FOR IMPROVING YOUR FRENCH

- ◆ In France see a film originally in English and dubbed into French; it's much easier to follow because the actors have to speak more carefully.

11

Not a B&B

If you feel that a B&B alone does not produce a sufficient income, you may want to engage in another activity as well. Or it may be the other way about: you already have another activity and are adding a B&B as a sideline. Either way you will have to work hard to give the guests the impression that they are receiving your undivided attention.

FARMING

This is where *Gîtes de France* came in and farmers still receive special treatment with favourable tax rates and increased grants. Staying on a working farm is immensely popular with both the British and the French and you will have an above-average occupancy rate. As a predominantly agricultural country right up to the 1960s, the French are much nearer their farming roots than other countries. They all like to think of themselves as farming folk. A difficulty for the fastidious Dutch and Americans is that farms do not always look like the idealised pictures. The reality is that it's a muddy and sometimes noisy business. It has to be said that Danish farms are the winners here. Where we stayed the buildings were freshly painted, there were no old cars, and the yard was swept morning and evening after the cows had been in for milking. My children still remember the pigs being born, and it was 25 years ago. Of course, not all farms have animals, at least not the ones you expect. Raising ostriches and llamas still come under the official heading of farming. The type of farm ought to be mentioned in the brochure.

This is one B&B in the country where there's no need for a pool. The surroundings would never be maintained anyway since farmers think gardening is for wimps. And exploit your privileged position by only taking guests for the week, Saturday to Saturday, no messing.

VITICULTURE

Viticulteurs (wine growers) are just as privileged as farmers, but more prestigious. A *chambres d'hôtes* run in conjunction with a vineyard will be very popular with both the French and foreigners. They will naturally expect to taste and buy the wines. It is particularly favoured by companies who run hiking, cycling and car itineraries, though these will be for one-night stays only. For hikers and cyclists, the company usually transports the luggage each day; picnic lunches may be required. *Gîtes de France* have a brochure *Séjours en Vignoble*, or contact one of the many firms who run this type of holiday. If not a *viticulteur* yourself, you could still run a *chambres d'hôtes* in a wine-growing area and make a special feature of visits to vineyards with wine tastings.

There are 12 areas of production:

L'Alsace	La Savoie et le Bugey
Le Beaujolais et le Lyonnais	Le Languedoc et le Roussillon
Le Bordelais	La Provence
La Bourgogne	Le Sud-Ouest
La Champagne	La Vallée de la Loire
Le Jura	La Vallée du Rhône et les Charentes

GITES, CHALETS, CAMPING

One or several *gîtes* are an excellent combination with a B&B. There is a lot of crossover of business both from the B&B to the *gîte* and vice versa. And all without paying for the advertising. However, this won't produce enough guests to fill a *gîte*, and certainly not for several. Unfortunately, *gîtes* need different advertising from a B&B. The only brochures that produce good results for both are *Chez Nous* and *Bonnes Vacances* (addresses in the Appendix).

If you only have one *gîte*, the best size is a small one-bedroom cottage for 2 people. This is because most of the guests in the B&B are couples. We had just such a *gîte* and there were people who stayed in the *gîte* and came back to the B&B, people who came to the B&B and came back the next year to the *gîte*, people who couldn't stay in the B&B because it was full and so took the *gîte*, people staying in the *gîte* had some friends come to the B&B for a few nights; in fact all sorts of permutations. **And** we could sometimes even use it as a B&B. So can you find a small corner somewhere to tuck a small *gîte*?

For a larger development of several *gîtes*, holiday chalets or a camp site, you should first discuss the project with the *Comité Départemental de Tourisme* of your department (address in telephone directory). Then discuss it with *Gîtes de France* and your *Direction Départementale de l'Equipement*, and then with the water and electricity companies. It's always possible there are constraints you didn't know about, and it will take many months to get planning permission. This is a large business requiring plenty of capital and administrative skills to run it profitably. Since a B&B is so labour intensive, are you sure you will be able to spare it the time?

Gîtes should be away from the main house for privacy and should each have their own private sitting-out space. Unless there are other outstanding attractions, you **must** have a pool. Some brochures won't even accept a property without one. I have seen properties advertised as being self-catering in July and August, and as a B&B for the rest of the year. I don't know that anyone has made this work because the ads I've seen soon disappear. It doesn't sound like a goer to me.

Gîtes and a B&B go so well together because the work for both is so similar. The bookings, the cleaning, the laundry, the being on hand for arrivals are common to both. You can provide linen, where absent owners find this difficult. If you have a *table d'hote* you can provide dinner. We found the *gîte* tenants usually took dinner at least once during their stay, and invariably came to the barbecues. One couple even had dinner every night. Some *gîte* owners offer dinner on the first night as an inducement; this wouldn't be difficult for you.

ACTIVITY HOLIDAYS

These are basically either sporting, or acquiring skills.

If you are offering the sport yourself, then you **must** be qualified in that speciality and possess all the right certificates. You need to decide whether these activities are an option for the guests generally, or a specialised week dedicated solely to that sport. For the former, you would mention it in your general advertising. For the latter you would have to advertise in the relevant sports magazines. You could, of course, offer the sport generally in the high season, with specialized weeks out of season. **Watch the capital expenditure.** Or you could feature sporting activities run by others. This is much the easier option and will reduce your insurance too.

Classes in languages, regional cookery, art, music, and many crafts can be run in conjunction with a B&B. There are many of them, so there is stiff competition. Most are run as a whole week's course, and are often held in the mid-season months. Really you need to be an experienced teacher of the subject concerned to give good value to the participants.

All activity holidays have some organising problems in common:

1. Which language? If in English, it excludes everyone else. It makes proceedings very slow if everything has to be said twice.

2. Many people will come as singles, so are there enough bedrooms or will they share?

3. A couple may have one partner who doesn't want to take part in the activity. What are they to do with their time?

4. Is it absolutely clear who provides the equipment and appropriate clothing? If someone arrives missing some items what will you do?

5. What if there are cancellations? What if only 2 people book? Would the activity still go ahead?

6. For outdoor activities what provision is there for bad weather?

7. If applicable: what about transport to the activity? What about transport for the usual free choice day?

8. In a workshop is the heating and lighting adequate?

9. What about laundry?

10. The general holiday brochures will not produce enough customers for special activities, so where will you advertise?

11. What will you do in the weeks when there is no activity scheduled? To run it as a conventional B&B would necessitate an additional set of advertising.

12. Are you absolutely confident it will pay?

Here are two case studies (*Fig. 33*) showing two completely different ways of running art classes. Case **A** is more of a hostel than a B&B and it has functioned well for many years. Case **B** has only just started, so one cannot say how well it will do. I am concerned that they are starting with such a lot of debt and they both have taken on a heavy work load. They could find themselves working 70 hours a week, which is not what they came to France for. I'm sure they will make changes – we all do – and will make it into a success.

OTHER POSSIBILITIES

Many a *ferme auberge* (country restaurant) has a B&B as well. Since the rooms are invariably reasonably priced and they serve excellent meals with home-produced specialities, they have a lot of appeal for a short stay.

	A	**B**
Previous career	Art teacher and practising artist	Commercial artist, no teaching experience
Reason for change	Retirement	On reaching 40 wanted to get away from 70-hour week
Family	Wife, no children still at home	Wife, 2 young children at private school
Property	Picturesque isolated stone farm buildings	1960's luxury stone-clad villa in elegant suburb of Mediterranean resort
Accommodation	Sleeps 24 in 11 bedrooms in farm buildings round a courtyard	Sleeps 8: 2 bedrooms in house, 2 in guest house, all with private patio
Bathrooms	Communal bathrooms	En-suite to each room
Grounds	Extensive former fields, good views, no pool	2-acre beautifully kept garden with 2 swimming pools
In wet weather	Barn	No provision
Art staff	1 other art teacher	He does all the teaching
Classes	No formal classes; students invited to put work up in barn for daily crit	Students taken to selected site every day in people carrier
Housekeeping	Wife supervises students who have to do a day's housekeeping + cooking every other day	Wife does all housekeeping plus all meals for full board
Advertising	Via art schools	Glossy brochure and web site
Period available	Summer only due to lack of heating	All year due to climate and central heating
Cost of property	Bought cheaply for cash	Very expensive, with mortgage
Renovation	Adding partitions, stairs, basic bathrooms, windows	En-suite bathrooms, + large amount on house as had not been well maintained
Cost of course and full board	Very cheap, aimed at all ages	Expensive, aimed at mature clients

Figure 33 Two case studies of very different art classes

On a campsite the B&B guests would be the superior ones because they are paying more for better accommodation. Only a summer activity, obviously.

Seminars would have to be very small and exclusive. There aren't many takers for this.

If you have serious catering experience, and a big suitable room, could you do weddings and functions generally? Or perhaps small groups for seminars, music tuition, all sorts of activities. For any form of music, dance or gymnastics you need a good semi-sprung wood floor which needs to be laid by a specialist.

NOT A *CHAMBRES D'HOTES*

Are you quite sure you want to be a *chambres d'hotes* at all? There are other interesting possibilities. *Gîtes de France* have the following categories:

Gîtes Panda	(children)
Gîtes d'Enfants	(children)
Gîtes d'Etape et de Séjour	(hostels and large gîtes)
Séjours à la Neige	(skiing)
Séjours Equestres	(riding)
Séjours Pêche	(fishing)
Séjours Vignoble	(vineyards)

They are all more hostels than B&Bs, but might suit your particular property and interests. To find out more, the best thing is to stay in one, or send the children as appropriate. You can be in one of these guides as well as the *chambres d'hôtes* guide, for an extra fee of course.

TIPS FOR MAKING IT PAY

- Advertise to reach the target customers.

- Do not take on anything for which you don't have the experience.

- Do not have too many special activities or expend too much capital until you are sure it is profitable.

- Have a back-up plan for when things go wrong.

- Have a party on the last night so that it's remembered as an enjoyable week that will be recommended to friends.

TIP FOR IMPROVING YOUR FRENCH

◆ In France join an art or craft class at a club or institute to practise conversation.

12

Publicity

To make a living, it is necessary to advertise **a lot**. Repeat bookings, word of mouth, friends and relatives from the UK, passing trade: none of these produce nearly enough customers. If there are 5 bedrooms, that's $5 \times 365 = 1{,}825$ nights a year and it takes a lot of effort even to fill half of it. To make full use of 3 or more bedrooms in the first year, it will probably take 25 per cent of you gross income, for the next few years 10 per cent, and should drop to 5 per cent when the business is established. In contrast, for 1 or 2 bedrooms it is best to limit the advertising cost to the absolute minimum, possibly even none at all. In the words of some actual proprietors in Chapter 13, you will see that their advertising does in fact run from 0 to appearing in over 20 guides (admittedly many of these at no cost). **Always** ask your guests where they found your name to judge the value of each outlet. Try a new one every year, but unfortunately you'll find it is possible for an advertisement not to produce a single response.

THE ORGANISATIONS

It is not compulsory to join one of the two government sponsored organisations, but there are many advantages. I do support the idea of everyone joining one organisation or the other, because in the UK we have the situation where few B&Bs belong to anything at all. Some are of very dubious quality and this reflects on the rest.

Gîtes de France
The advantages are:

1. An entry in their widely distributed guides.
2. Listing by tourist offices.
3. Advice and information when starting up.
4. Possibility of obtaining a grant.
5. Inspection and a grading system.
6. Use of their nationally known logo.
7. Meeting with other proprietors and exchanging views.
8. An optional reservation centre (15 per cent commission).
9. Help with disputes and legal assistance if required.
10. A quarterly magazine with helpful articles.

There is a branch in the chief town of each *département*, and as they are run very autonomously and set their own fees, it is not possible to give entry and annual costs. Ask at your tourist office for the address of the appropriate branch. There are about 8,000 *chambres d'hôtes* members, a figure which is rising year by year, with an average of 2½ bedrooms each. This is a very small number of rooms per owner and means that they are essentially an organisation for those looking for a secondary income. Only a few have the maximum number of 6 bedrooms. About ⅓ of members have a *table d'hôte*. The organisation was originally founded for *gîte* owners and the fact that this word still appears in the title does cause some confusion even for the French.

Four types of *chambres d'hôtes* guide are published:

National	Each department
Each region	Prestige (selection only)

Their inspection and grading system is widely used as a benchmark by other guides so it is **imperative** to be in the right grade for the establishment you hope to run. The grades run from *1* to *4 épis* (ears of corn). *3 épis* is by far the most common grade and you should aim for **at least** this. *1 épi* and *2 épis* **must be avoided**; you'll not get anywhere. If, by any chance, you are awarded less than *3 épis,* call on the tourist office to help find out what is required for a better grade. Do everything necessary, then ask for a re-grading and have the tourist office present. *4 épis* are absolutely fine if you can make it, but it will take a very high standard all round. For the inspection, the rooms must be fully furnished and with a sample breakfast laid out. This has to take place before June to get into the following year's guide, so it is scarcely possible to feature in it for the first year of opening. Premises are only re-inspected every 5 years. In fact the grading system has come in for a lot of criticism, as they admit in their magazine. The result has been the inauguration of an anonymous inspection team, but only in limited areas so far. It is not actually necessary to register all the rooms with *Gîtes de France*, though they won't like me telling you that.

Some departments have additional specialist guides, for example:- 'Gîtes Senior' or 'Gîtes de Jardin'. You will be invited to be in them if appropriate.

Most branches have an annual meeting, followed by a jolly meal where the real business takes place. You make friends with the other owners and exchange horror stories like, 'There was this couple who were cooking a meal in their bedroom on a camping gaz stove'. Looked at simply as the number of customers received in return for the annual fee, it is good value. You will be asked to fill in endless surveys.

Clévacances

The 1980s and 1990s produced an explosion in the number of *gîtes* and *chambres d'hôtes* and the government became concerned that so many were totally outside any fiscal or inspection regime. *Clévacances* was set up as an alternative to *Gîtes de France* for those who don't want to join the larger organisation, and they already have 2,000 *chambres d'hôtes* members. It is run by local tourist offices, who carry out the inspections and fix the charges.

They have a similar grading system to *Gîtes de France*; but theirs is *1* to *4 clés* (keys). They also help with obtaining grants, and produce a good brochure. Go and discuss your B&B proposals with the tourist office, whichever organisation you are thinking of joining.

ADVERTISING IN BED & BREAKFAST GUIDES

There are many of them, but only about a dozen that have a large enough sale or distribution to be really effective, and new ones come and go frequently. So be cautious before committing any fees and read the small print carefully. It is known for publishers to make their income from selling the advertising space and not from selling the book. Though if the entry is free there's unlikely to be anything to lose. The guides distributed free are only used in the first year; those paid for are normally kept for 3 years, so the business builds up year by year. Our extreme was someone using a 6-year-old edition. Have a good spread of nationalities.

The presentation of your entry divides into two broad formats: those guides who write it themselves, and those where you have complete control. If writing it themselves, you must have been visited, and sometimes they make mistakes which are hugely annoying. For designing the advertisement yourself, you must take great care, and unfortunately much of the work has to be done in the high season. But it's essential not to miss the deadlines. After the photograph, it's the wording in bold print that grabs attention.

Follow these tips:

1. Push the establishment's key features.

2. Avoid flowery language and keep to the facts.

3. Be truthful and don't exaggerate.

4. Mention the warm welcome or personal attention, and any features 'new this year'.

5. Be brief in describing the locality and concentrate on the property.

6. Give a contact name.

A Selection of guides

Recommended names are shown in heavy type.

Organisation	Name of guide	Address	Nationality
AA	Bed & Breakfast in France	Fanum House, Basingstoke, Hants RG21 4EA, UK 01256 491545	British
B&B France	Bed & Breakfast (France)	9 rue Jaques Louvel-Tessier 75010 Paris, France 01 42 01 34 34 www.bedbreak.com	Br/Fr
Alistair Sawday	French Bed & Breakfast	44 Ambra Vale East, Bristol BS8 4RE, UK 0117 929 9921	British
Bonnes Vacances	Bonnes Vacances	The Old Brewery, Vincent Lane, Dorking, Surrey RH4 3HQ, UK 01582 814254 www.bvdirect.co.uk	
Chez Nous	France	Spring Mill, Earby, Barnoldswick, Lancashire BB94 0AA 0870 444 6600 www.cheznous.com	British
Clévacances	Locations en France	54 bd de l'Embouchure, 31022 Toulouse, France 05 61 13 55 66 www.clevacances.com	French
Filipacchi	130 Chambres d'Hôtes	Hachette Editions, 43 quai Grenelle, 75015 Paris, France 01 43 92 30 00	French

Gîtes de France	Chambres et Tables d'Hôtes	59 rue St-Lazare, 75439 Paris, France 01 49 70 75 75 www.gitesdefrance.fr	French
Hotels Abroad	Hotels Abroad	5 Worlds End Lane, Orpington, Kent BR6 6AA, UK 01689 882 500 www.hotelsabroad.com	British
Karen Brown	Charming Bed & Breakfasts	PO Box 70, San Mateo, CA 94401, USA www.karenbrown.com	USA
Maisons de France	Maisons de France	Crehunault, 22630 Evran, France 02 96 82 25 97 www.lesmaisonsdefrance.com	Irish
Michelin	1,000 Hotels and Charming Places to Stay	33 St James Square, London SW1Y 4JS www.michelin-travel.com	French
Le Petit Futé	Les 1001 Meilleures Chambres d'Hôtes	—	French
Rivages	Maisons d'Hôtes de Charme	106 bd Saint-Germain, 75006 Paris, France 01 44 41 39 90	French
Routard	Tables et Chambres à la Campagne	22 Passage Boiton 75013 Paris, France www.routard.com	French
Wolsey Lodges	Wolsey Lodges	9 Market Place, Hadleigh, Ipswich, Suffolk IP7 5DL, UK 01473 822058 www.wolsey-lodges.co.uk	British

Notes

AA – the Automobile Association with its vast marketing resources. In association with *Gîtes de France*.

Bonnes Vacances – for £495 (plus VAT) for ¼-page this is good value for B&B as well as gîtes.

Chez Nous – belongs to the giant Thompson Travel. At £407 for ⅛-page and £754 for ¼-page (plus VAT) this is by far the most expensive of all. But it works for B&B as well as gîtes.

Clévacances – members only.

Gîtes de France – members only.

Hotels Abroad – you may think this is out of your league, but it really does include B&Bs with only 3 bedrooms. Best for 1-night stays.

Karen Brown – all the hype of an American firm. Good for mid-season clients. In association with Gîtes de France.

Maisons de France – a niche market.

Michelin – The vast marketing resources of the well known map maker.

Rivages – upmarket guide for the best properties. No fee. Very popular in Belgium.

Routard – the no.1 guide for the French. Classified entry only, no pictures. No fee. In association with Gîtes de France, entry by invitation only.

MAGAZINES, NEWSPAPERS, DIRECTORIES

The following magazines have all produced good results:

France, Digbeth Street, Stowe-On-The-Wold, Glos. GL54 1BN. Tel: 01451 831398

The Lady, 39-40 Bedford Street, London WC2E 9ER. Tel: 020 7379 4717

The Oldie, 65 Newman Street, London W1T 3EG. Tel: 020 7565 3188

You can either have a classified or a larger entry. They do have rather a short shelf life, but are useful if you have missed the autumn deadlines for the main guides.

In-house and specialist magazines can be used, nothing lost if they are free, but they do have a small readership and even smaller number of people just happening to be planning a trip to France and staying in a B&B.

The daily newspapers and their travel supplements are expensive and have the shortest shelf life of all, but try a classified entry and see if it works.

You may be solicited to appear in various trade directories, I doubt if it's worth it. And that goes for paying for an entry in the *Yellow Pages* too, because *chambres d'hôtes* are put under *gîtes* and no one thinks of looking there.

PHOTOGRAPHS

Customers will have chosen the area and price before searching for a particular establishment. Once they start to look at advertisements, it's the photograph that makes the greatest impact. You may also want additional pictures for the brochure or web pages. Employ a professional if possible; the cost will be recovered in extra bookings. But if taking them yourself, here are some tips:

1. Choose the time of day when the view is in full sunlight and the sky is blue.

2. Avoid evening and winter.

3. If you have a pool, a picture is essential, even at extra cost for another photograph in the guide.

4. Take pictures of any other attractive features of the property such as the garden, beamed interiors, large fireplace.

5. Place something on the bed such as books, magazines, pile of towels or a peignoir.

6. Open shutters, close windows, and remove all clutter.

7. Add a garden table and chairs. Place some fruit, flowers or tray of drinks on the table.

8. Flowers are always winners. Add hanging baskets, window-boxes or large pots with flowers. Take a view of the property with sunflowers, wisteria or blossom if possible.

9. Experiment with climbing up a ladder. A particularly good idea for interior views.

10. Don't include people, but animals are acceptable.

Always keep the publicity material and photos handy; you never know when there might be an opening.

THE WEB

The web should be an adjunct to advertising in bed and breakfast guides, not a substitute. It is fine for those people who already have a good idea of what they want, but the printed pages of a book are still the best for browsing. On the advertisement customers can be directed to the web site for further information.

All the guides mentioned have their own web sites which are being used more and more. And you will be solicited to appear on many others, for a fee of course. Resist them all until you have a reliable recommendation. However, more and more proprietors do have their own web site. You may have to pay someone to design it.

A good specialist site is:

   www.frenchconnections.co.uk

People who make a preliminary enquiry by email can be directed to your web page for further information instead of sending them a brochure. This is a great saving because the number of firm bookings resulting from each enquiry goes down year by year. A booking form that can be printed and sent with the deposit completes the ensemble.

But, in this high-tech age, don't forget that your clients are more likely to be over 50 than below, and they just might not have a computer.

BROCHURE AND STATIONERY

For one or two bedrooms, do you really need a brochure? An elegant visiting card is more sophisticated than a leaflet on thin paper. Or have a card of the format ⅓ of an A4 sheet. This fits neatly into a standard envelope and would contain just the name, address, possibly a map, and a space for writing in the price by hand.

With several bedrooms, a well designed brochure is **essential**. It will pay to have it professionally designed, but it won't pay for each copy to cost too much. If they cost more than £1 each you will be inhibited from distributing them freely. They either need to be professionally printed, or can you produce a good job with a desk-top printer?

Checklist of the information that should be included:

Front page

1. Drawing or photo of the building or an interesting part of it.

2. Name of establishment.

3. What you do:
    i.e. Chambres d'Hôtes/Bed & Breakfast
    or Maison d'Hôtes/Country Guest House
    (+Table d'Hôte).

4. Name of town, village or region + 'France'.

5. *Gîtes de France* or *Clévacances* logo if you belong.

Interior

6. A few words of description of your establishment (don't be too long winded), include number of bedrooms and 'all rooms with en-suite bathroom'.

7. Don't be shy about mentioning a small detail that could put you ahead of the competition, such as: Champagne aperitif before dinner on Saturdays, fresh flowers in the bedroom, a branded special soap. It gives a very good impression.

8. Where appropriate, mention dinners and lunches and show a sample menu or give distance to nearest restaurant.

9. Describe the swimming pool and other amenities, preferably with pictures.

10. Brief description of places to visit and sports facilities nearby.

11. A few items of essential information such as: policies on children/animals/smoking/and dates of closure.

12. Preferably have pictures of a bedroom and the dining-room.

13. Mention any other activities such as '*gîtes*' or 'working farm'.

14. Mention any other languages you speak.

Last page

15. Thumbnail diagram of France with a dot to show where you are.

16. Location map of the immediate vicinity and the nearest village. It's the last 5 miles that really matter, Michelin will cope with the rest.

17. The words 'For further information contact':
    Name of proprietor
    Full address, phone/fax, (+email and web).

To get all the above on, the usual format is an A4 sheet folded in three. The brochure should either be in French and English, plus any other language of course, or have a separate one for each (watch the cost). If in both languages, the English can be just a brief translation. The translation into French **must** be done by a French national; if you don't know anyone ask the tourist office. You will see I have suggested 'country guest house' as a possible alternative to 'bed & breakfast', which may be a better translation if you have several bedrooms with *table d'hôte*. It's best to have the price list on a separate sheet which is inserted into the folded brochure, then it can be changed every year. Ask a friend to look over the brochure layout before having 300 printed; it's amazing what can get left out.

You will also need headed writing paper, set up on the computer of course, if you have one, and visiting cards. Ideally there should be a uniformity of style between these and the brochure because they will often be sent out together. Sooner or later you will be solicited to have a photo of your place on a postcard, and these are a good promotional idea.

OUTDOOR SIGNS

It's a big complaint of customers that B&Bs are not well-signposted. When clients get lost on a hot day after a long drive, they arrive cross, and that's not a good start. You will have noticed a somewhat more relaxed attitude to signs in France compared to the UK. You need something in the centre of your village, and at every turning until your establishment is reached. I warn you, the arrangements are a little informal. Then you can have a sign 300 metres away from your entrance in both directions by right. Standard signs are available from road sign manufacturers; ask at the *Direction Départementale de l'Equipement* for an address as they are ordering all the time. Or you may prefer something more individual with your name on; get quotes from a firm listed under *Signalisation* in the *Yellow Pages*.

Then you need a sign at your entrance, and its size depends on how commercial you want to be: large if you want to attract passing trade, discreet otherwise. Both *Gîtes de France* and *Clévacances* **insist** that members display their logo at the entrance. **Never** have a home-made sign, it looks very amateurish. Unfortunately, painted signs on wood don't last beyond a couple of years unless protected by an overhanging roof.

OTHER POSSIBILITIES

There are a number of ways to advertise for free. Don't neglect them.

First is your tourist office. Keep it supplied with brochures, and keep in touch with the personnel to remind them of your existence. You can also leave brochures in all the other centres in your *département* if you think it worth it. But in another *département* they either won't be accepted or a fee will be required which is unlikely to be worthwhile.

Next comes leaving your visiting cards with all other likely looking establishments: restaurants, estate agents, tourist shops, sports clubs. Hotels are likely to be a bit sniffy about a B&B.

Join some clubs to get known; there is a lot of local business to be picked up. Also get to know all the other *chambres d'hôtes* owners in the vicinity so that you can pass on customers between you when full.

One day I saw a name and the words '*chambres d'hôtes*' signwritten on the door of a 4WD. I mentally saluted that owner as being very businesslike. The moral is to keep an eye open for possibilities.

REPEAT BUSINESS AND RECOMMENDATIONS

One always hopes that guests will recommend you and come back themselves another time – it's very satisfying. And as your name gets known it means you can advertise less. But don't expect too much; it doesn't happen often enough to fill the rooms, and anyway we are all very restless these days. We don't often go back to the same place.

Our repeat business grew year by year, but many were not strictly holidaymakers. They were friends or relatives of people living nearby, attending local sporting events, or househunting/renovating/moving in.

You could send a 'thank you' note after guests leave, a Christmas card to the British, or a New Year's card to the French; and even include a photo taken during their stay: only if they're people you want back, of course. Don't omit the people who enquired but didn't come. But just be a little cautious who you contact afterwards; it isn't always welcome. One proprietor returned a pair of black lace knickers to the address given, only to receive them back again with a note: 'These are not mine'.

BUSINESS NAME

The business name needs careful thought. Within a village there will be a road name and a number exactly the same as in the UK, so you need a name for the enterprise. Have a sign made and hung at right angles to the street. In the country the situation differs. There are **no road names**, only road numbers and it does make addresses difficult to find. Instead there is the *lieu-dit* (literally 'place called'), which featured on the deeds. This is the official name of the land, not the house. If there are 10 houses on the same parcel of land, they all have the same name.

Since the *lieu-dit* is the official name, it cannot be changed; but you can use any name you like for business purposes. Unless the property is a local landmark such as a château, or a mill, there are advantages in choosing a suitable business name. Looking far ahead to when you retire, you have either got something more to put in the basket of goodies when you sell as a going concern, or you take the sign down and are free of people knocking on the door for the next five years and wanting a bed for the night. The name would go above the *lieu-dit* as the address.

Tips for choosing a business name:

1. With the help of a French speaker choose a dozen possibles.
2. Consider using the name of your village or something relating to its history, and a feature of the area could be used as a logo.
3. Avoid names that are difficult to pronounce in French or English.
4. Do not include any words in English.
5. Long names are difficult to fit on a sign.
6. Choose an unusual word or the search engines will report dozens of examples.
7. Many lists are in alphabetical order, so you should be near the beginning.
8. Consult another French person to double check that the one chosen is suitable. You don't want to be mistaken for a retirement home or religious institution.

To tie it all together, you now need a logo; nothing fancy, just the name always in the same type face. It should be the same on everything: outdoor signs, brochure, letter head, visiting cards. Add a little symbol such as a feature of the building, tree, bird or animal only if you are confident to do it. Then scan it into the computer and use it on everything.

CHEQUES VACANCES

This is a scheme on the lines of luncheon vouchers, but is for holidays, restaurants and some leisure activities. They are given to employees by large French companies. The client pays with the vouchers and you claim the money back from the organisation. You have to be a member, but as it costs nothing you might as well. They only take 1 per cent commission. (See Appendix for the address.)

THE FIRST YEAR

This is the most difficult of all, and if the business is sparse, it is very discouraging. Firstly: were you able to get into any guides the previous autumn? If a photo of the outside was impossible, then perhaps one of a bedroom. If you did not achieve that, then it will have to be a web page or magazines or newspapers which have later publishing dates. Whatever the method, it **must** be published by mid-January if you are to have any sort of season at all. Naturally you will be frantically busy getting the place ready, but speed and effort are essential. Do not put up a sign and **wait** for the business to take off by itself. (*For a glossary of publicity terms, see Fig. 34.*)

agenda (m)	diary	droit d'entrée (m)	enrolment fee
annonce (f)	advertisment	épi (m)	ear of corn
petite annonce (f)	classified ad	guide (f)	guide
bôite aux lettres (f)	letter box	panneau (m)	outdoor sign
brochure (f)	brochure	*Pages Jaunes* (f)	*Yellow Pages*
carte (f)	map	rendez-vous (m)	appointment
carte de visite (f)	visiting card	renseignements (m)	information
coordonnées (f)	address, etc.	réunion (f)	meeting
cotisation (f)	subscription	syndicat d'initiative (m)	tourist office
dépliant (m)	leaflet		

Figure 34   Glossary

TIPS FOR MAKING IT PAY

◆ Advertise a lot.
◆ Plan your advertising early.
◆ Advertise to attract different nationalities.

TIP FOR IMPROVING YOUR FRENCH

◆ Write a business letter in French.

13

The Staff

YOURSELVES

Imagine yourself in the guests' place for a moment. They get out of their carriage to find a warm welcome, the beds made, the fires lit, and a meal will shortly be put on the table; and all without any effort on their part. Could be a scene from a costume drama set a hundred years ago, couldn't it? I'm not saying that they are the nobs and you are the servants; we're all egalitarian now. But what you are really offering is a house with servants. For one night or fourteen nights, the guests' expectation is that they have paid to be waited on. Though one big difference between now and then is that now you own the house, not them, and this alters the balance considerably. Let us just say that nowadays 'looked after' can be substituted for 'waited on'. To give the feel of how this situation originated, I have included 'Mrs Beeton's Book of Household Management' in the book list in the Appendix; not for the recipes, but do read the section on servants.

In very grand houses there was a servant for everything, even a 'boots'. I'm glad we don't polish trainers, or we'd be doing that too. As it is, the 1 or 2 or 3 of you are chambermaid, cleaner, cook, washer-upper, gardener, receptionist, computer techie, financial manager, advertising manager, secretary, purchasing officer, upholsterer, laundry maid, plumber, electrician, waiter, painter and decorator – to name only a few. We ran an ambulance service once, too, when a guest had to go to hospital at 4am.

What are the hours? Well, the latest any guest arrived back at night was 5am (they had been to a wedding), and the earliest any guest left in the morning was 5am (to avoid the heat and traffic on a long journey). Fortunately these events were exceptional, and you aren't expected to be around. But someone does need to be around between 7am and 11pm; if one of the partners is a lark and the other an owl then the hours can be staggered to suit. You should be able to get a reasonable break in the middle of the day, though between 13.30 and 14.00 is a favourite time for the French to phone. I hope I've not presented too daunting a picture, because the above only applies to the high season. Mid-season will mostly be easier, unless you have a group. And October to Easter you'll be lucky to have many guests at all, unless you're a ski resort. Not that you can rest. There's everything to be got ready for next season, but at least you can work at your own pace.

For holidays, the best months to go away are November and December. In January and February there will be a lot of enquiries and bookings. March is only alright if you can have your phone and emails attended to by someone else. This person needs to be familiar with the business.

You will acclimatise much more quickly to living abroad by wholly accepting all things French than by constantly popping 'home' for the things you can't do without. Have a French car, use a French dentist, and you will soon find there's a French equivalent for 90% of your favourite British foods.

RELATIVES AND FRIENDS

They'll all want to visit in the first year. You won't be too busy (except with the DIY), so that's not a problem. After that you'll have to make some rules if they're not to fill the guest rooms in high season. You could designate a 'family week' in which you don't accept any visitors and can then devote your full time to the family. The last week of August would be a good choice as it's not as popular as the first 3 weeks. Or for friends generally you could say that if they come in high season they have to pay full rate, and you won't be able to spare them any time. But if they come out of season you'll have more time and there will be no charge. I would be very cautious if anyone says they will come as a 'working party'. It will cost **at least** £30 a week to feed them.

CHILDREN

If you have dependent children the finances of the business must be taken very seriously. Few B&Bs produce a family size income. So either the business must be expanded beyond just a B&B, or one of the parents must take an outside job. The latter leaves only one person to look after the children and run the B&B as well. Up to three rooms will be manageable; for more rooms you'll only cope if you don't do dinners or you have plenty of help. Of course children of 10 and over should make excellent slave labour in the summer.

HELP IN THE HOUSE

A *femme de ménage* (cleaning lady) is the obvious first choice. There's such a lot to be done. Seven mornings a week would be nice, but most of us have to settle for less; and anyway there's the maximum 35-hour working week. Also no one wants to work on Sunday. Since this is necessarily a morning job it precludes anyone still in education unless it were just for the holidays. The second choice is for someone to help with the dinners and this is more flexible. Many people in France take a second job. We were surprised to see the electrician, who had been fixing our fuse box in the morning, behind a bar in the evening.

Employing workers is absolutely full of red tape and extra expense on top of their pay packet. The salary has to be at least the *SMIC* (minimum wage), currently €7.19 per hour, and the government takes a contribution of more than 40%. The social security costs borne by the employer are the highest in the world.

There are two schemes to reduce the burden of the paperwork: '*chèque emploi*' for businesses, and '*chèque emploi service*' for households. The first is for employees working less than 8 hours a week or less than 1 month a year. The second is for domestic help **only**, and the person **must not** work in the business. But since you'll never have time to look after your own quarters in high season, this could be useful. Ask your bank to set either one up. Both do indeed make life much simpler, and I wish the UK would take up the idea.

How do you find your reliable, clean, hardworking, honest treasure? With difficulty is the answer. Ask other ex-pats, or that fount of local gossip: your hairdresser. At the interview, the following points need to be covered:

- Which days to come. If you need them on Saturday this is the **first** thing to establish.

- The pay.

- The hours. The French do not normally work between 12.00 and 14.00 hours.

- Will they be taking off for their own holiday in July or August? This is **crucial. Will they work over the August 15th holiday?**

- If there are young children, what arrangements will be made for them?

- You could always ask if they would be willing to take the ironing home with them (only if they have a car of course).

- It's only fair to say if the job is temporary, i.e. finishing at the end of September.

- Ask for at least 2 references, from other ex-pats if possible, then be sure to follow them up.

I expect you will be asked for a bit more than the minimum wage for a regular morning cleaning person. Confirm all the above in writing, presumably in French (you'll have to do your best). If they are young and still at school, be very, very, wary if you are intending to pay them. Has their mother taught them how to make a bed or clean a bathroom? If in any doubt, the best thing is to say they can come for a trial period, though if it doesn't work out, you can be in a real fix, with the season started, and no help. One quirk of the indigenous population is that their stomachs all rumble at precisely midday. In fact you've got to be a long way out in the country to be out of earshot of the hooters that sound off at this hour. Midday is sacrosanct as the lunch hour. This is not very convenient when the guests have ignored your requirement to leave by 10am, and are still around at 11. How are you ever to get the rooms done?

The number of days a cleaning person needs to come will depend on how often the rooms are serviced. You will find the weekends particularly busy. Although you are not a *gîte* with a fixed changeover day of Saturday, you will find that many guests do choose to arrive on this day, and then of course no one wants to work on Sundays.

You can use their first name for a cleaning person, but for other tradesmen use their surname at least at first; and you only shake hands the first time you meet, not every day. My cleaning lady said I was much too polite, she never got 'please' and 'thank you' when working in a hotel. I kept to the British way.

If you have imported friends or relatives from the UK to help out, where are they going to sleep? They certainly can't have one of the guest rooms, and it can't be a sofa for 6 weeks or more. Failing any room in the house, and since it's summer, the options are: a caravan, a summer house, or a minimum conversion in an ancillary building. With all of these, the sanitary arrangements will be difficult. Even though it's warm, there can be terrific storms with 10 minutes of torrential rain, so camping isn't really an option for someone who has to work.

SPECIALIST AND GARDENING HELP

A reliable electrician and plumber who will come at short notice are **essential**, unless you have the skills yourself. If not skilled at DIY, you will also need a jobbing builder who will turn up quickly in emergencies. As self-employed people, they will present a bill in the usual manner.

For doing defined jobs in the grounds, there should be no difficulty in finding someone to do it on a contract basis, or they may charge by the hour, but either way they are not directly employed by you. For employing a regular gardener either of the two cheque systems could be used. That is, if you can find someone. This is difficult because most men either have a regular job, or cannot cope with heavy work. You might, with luck, find a lady. As well as the usual gardening, they may need to look after the swimming pool, the bicycles, the stock of logs and any animals.

DOING BUSINESS WITH THE FRENCH

We found the French, on the whole, friendly and helpful. They are normally extremely polite. But I regret the world of business is rougher and tougher than the normal tourist encounters. French is a wonderful language for being rude. As a foreigner with a funny accent, you are an obvious target, though I doubt that it actually amounts to many more occasions than in the UK. Don't take it to heart. It'll be forgotten the next time you meet. You will get further and meet less resistance if you don't try to be too British all the time. Speak in French as much as possible, learn the correct forms of address, and don't put up notices in your establishment in English only.

The French can seem exasperatingly inefficient at times and you wonder how the *TGV* or *Concorde* ever got built. A letter arrives fixing an appointment for yesterday; someone arrives an hour late at a big meeting with no apology; Christmas decorations in a restaurant are still there in February. Just relax and accept that we northern Europeans and Americans perhaps value efficiency **for its own sake**; the southerners care about the end product, but **not** the means of getting there.

Among country people there is a great element of helping each other. Don't be afraid to ask for help and always accept it, if possible, when offered. Don't try to pay, or give any sort of 'thank you' gift. Just be prepared to help them out on some future occasion. The system works like savings in the bank; it's there when you need it and you will learn and gain a lot.

KEEPING UP THE STANDARD

Without any hotel experience, it's hard to know just what level of service is required. Well, it should be below a 4-star hotel. The chocolate on the pillow at night, toilet paper folded to a V-shape, trouser press: all these belong to a more pretentious establishment. Yet you must not be too informal and homely. Bars of soap that have been used by someone else, cleaning materials left lying about, personal clothes left hanging in a cupboard: these won't do. Not all *chambres d'hôtes* undertake to 'service' (that means clean and make the beds) every day. If not, you would have to explain what to expect. Even if it's done on all other days, Sunday is particularly difficult. People are apt to stay around, so either you do the minimum or tell them 'not on Sundays' and they'll probably accept that. I've known hotels not accept new arrivals on Sundays but it would mean a loss of business.

It's hard to remember, but you **must** knock on bedroom doors and **wait** for an answer before entering, for obvious reasons. In your attire there's a difference between being casual and being sloppy. The universal jeans or shorts with T-shirt are fine for daytime, but you should change for dinner if you are serving. You will find that most of the guests change.

MANAGING YOUR TIME

If it all sounds like a great deal of hard work, well, it is in high season, therefore you must stop doing it all to impossible standards and wearing yourself out. Probably you came to France for the easy lifestyle, and here you are working 18-hour days. Examine everything to see if the work could be reduced, or the time spent carrying out things about could be cut. Give yourself a proper break after lunch. Could the administration be reduced by more use of the computer? Could the cooking time be reduced, not by buying in products, but by timing the recipes and seeing which are quickest to prepare? Give yourself some privacy. With a couple of bedrooms there aren't too many people to worry about, but beyond that you could feel pressured. We had an objection to notices saying *privé* (private) at first. But, as the number of bedrooms climbed, we did put one on the kitchen door and on the door to our accommodation.

In the season the proprietor's day will look something like this if you do dinners (though not so neatly compartmentalised):

7–10am	Attending on guests and their breakfast, gardening
10–12.30	Housework, laundry, general maintenance
12.30–2.30pm	Relax
2.30–4pm	Some pre-prep for dinner, office work, ironing
4–5pm	Talking to guests and new arrivals
5–10pm	Preparing, serving, clearing guests' dinner
10–11pm	Tidying and locking up

If you have paid help, delegate. Let them get on with it. Give the cleaning person a list of the rooms to be cleaned *à fond* (thoroughly) for a changeover, and those to be tidied for people staying on. Then you must not be bothered any more. If there's no initiative to see what's needed, this isn't the right person. Don't ask her to come back next year. Tell the garden person the end result required and let them get on with it. Don't hover.

THE PROPRIETORS

To give the true flavour of what it is like to run a *chambres d'hôtes*, I asked five proprietors to speak into a recording machine and tell me how it seems to them. It's noticeable how different they all are. In fact, one has now retired after 10 years, three are in the thick of it, and one is just about to start. Here they are:

Anne

Anne and her husband bought their charming old mill house in 1989 and ran it as a *chambres d'hôtes* for ten years. They had 6 bedrooms, a 1-bedroom *gîte* and a large garden with a swimming pool. They did not have a *table d'hôte*. Now they are retired.

After spending all our holidays in France we decided we liked the country so much we would retire there. However, we couldn't wait that long and, at 50, with our children gone to university, we decided to look for a suitable property to run as a *chambres d'hôtes* because we were too young to be completely retired. We found an old mill, very beautiful, habitable, but with possibility for renovation. So we arrived on my 50th birthday. There was an enormous amount of renovation, but we had our first guests, French, after 3 months.

Our mill was in a classified site so any exterior work had to be approved by the architect. My husband was very expert at building work. We had a French electrician and plumber, to help get things done quickly. It's good to employ French because we're living in their country. We did get a bit uptight when English or other nationalities come and bring their own materials for their workers from their own country.

Our guests were European, American, Russian, Australian. We got on very well with the French, and the locals accepted us and thought we were doing a good job. We opened the first winter, but there wasn't really any custom, and after 2 winters we decided only to open from Easter to October. The winters were spent decorating, building and preparing for the following year. If we did have a holiday, which was rare, that was at the end of the season in November. We went to Spain. When guests arrived we greeted them with smiles, even if it was raining, and a drink. Always smiling. Always smiling.

It was very expensive to employ anybody, so I had to do all the cleaning and the laundry, the changing of towels every day, the hanging on the line. My husband had to do all the grounds, the swimming pool, the general maintenance. That was onerous because we had too much land and Englishmen like to keep their lawns mown. The bookings and administration were difficult during the season because you're also serving meals, drinks, smiling, and trying to answer the phone at the same time. We didn't have a great deal of trouble with the French tax, health insurance, etc., because we had registered and found the Chamber of Commerce very helpful.

We didn't belong to *Gîtes de France*. We were told we were too much like a hotel to be a *chambres d'hôtes*, and too much like a *chambres d'hôtes* to be a hotel. So I suppose we were a guest house. We advertised with *Chez Nous* and the *Sunday Times*. Word of mouth of course is very important.

We had high moments and low moments: trees falling down, electricity supplies cut. We had our own spring, and if the electricity was cut there was no water, but everybody seemed to understand. We had just lovely people. Lots of wonderful memories, but we reached 60 and decided that was enough. No regrets. Go for it; it's very rewarding if you're prepared to work hard.

Tony

Tony and his wife have run a *chambres d'hôtes* and *table d'hôte* for 13 years in a house in the centre of a medieval bastide town. They bought the house in 1990. There are 6 bedrooms, of which one is for the disabled on the ground floor, and a small garden for the guests' use. His wife had experience of hotel work before they came to France.

We'd always intended to open a small hotel or a *chambres d'hôtes*, but we plumped for a *chambres d'hôtes* as it is the ideal way of keeping a hands-on business. The *immoblier* advised that if we wanted an all-year-round business, it would not succeed in the country as we originally intended. We arrived before retirement age and had to make a living. Due to problems before we left, we arrived in France with only £2,000 in the bank. The result was we had to take out a mortgage. So we didn't exactly start off in a good way.

We had very little French then and I went to a few classes, but we learnt more by sitting at the dinner table with our French clients and a French/English dictionary. We had quite a few entertaining evenings learning French. Answering the phone was a big problem, but after you've had the phone banged down several times because people couldn't understand, it focuses your mind wonderfully when you've got to earn a living. So we picked up French pretty quickly.

The property was in a good state when we bought it, but we had to put in 6 bathrooms. We had minimal problems with the building work, mainly because we did a lot of it ourselves. I think it's fair to say that you always have some problems with officialdom, but we'd run a small business in Britain and our experience is that problems are below the level with officials there.

We get on very well with the French, no problems that way at all. 60% of our guests are French, 20% English, and this year already we have had American and Australian, worldwide trade literally. In the 13 years we've been running the business, I can only think of less than 10 times where we had a particular problem, and only twice have had to ask clients to leave. We do have problems with children. A *table d'hôte*, where everybody eats together is extremely reliant on the ambience. We do find the French and most of the other European children behave and are quite OK with the meals. But we find that Dutch and British children are an exception, in particular the British. This has caused a degree of embarrassment to us.

We have all-the-year-round business, though in winter it is probably 50% of what we achieve in July and August. We always seem to have 2 or 3 bedrooms occupied. When there are no reservations we'll have a weekend in Spain or the Pyrenees. We very rarely visit the UK except when we have to: weddings, illnesses, funerals. The main reason is it's quite horrendous how expensive it is.

We don't mind getting up to do the breakfasts except when people say they particularly want breakfast at 7, roll down at 8, spend an hour having breakfast, and eventually we have to remind them that they should have left at 11. We find that people do occasionally take advantage. (This is Tony's wife speaking: The cooking isn't a problem. Our menus are French, but at first I wasn't au fait with the local cooking and a neighbour taught me. The only thing is that dinners happen at the end of the day and it is tiring.)

I did find the housekeeping onerous at the beginning, but then I'd spent 5 years in the Air Force so it wasn't too difficult. I'm pleased we haven't got a swimming pool. We plan the garden for minimum maintenance. The bookkeeping we leave entirely to the accountant. We're not computer oriented at all.

We've never found French tax, health insurance, or social security difficult. But I think others could well have a different story. If we've got queries on tax, we go to the tax authorities direct, because they're the ones who decide. It doesn't matter if you've had an English adviser telling you that you don't do this or you don't do that. If the tax inspector at the local level says you pay it, you pay it. I think you pay an enormous amount for so called expert advice outside the system.

Advertising was difficult at the beginning because we were strapped for cash, so we first got into the *Guide de Routard*, and we soon found that we were getting into other guides, and now we're in 20, none of which do we pay for, unless we want a picture. So we spend about £600 a year.

I wouldn't have any hesitation in saying that it's an excellent way to earn a living if you want to come to France.

Shelagh

Shelagh, her husband and her sister run a *chambres d'hôtes* with *table d'hôte* in the country near one of the *Plus Beaux Villages de France*. It has 5 bedrooms at present, and they are preparing a 6th bedroom for next season. They bought the house with a derelict barn in 1998 and her husband, a builder by trade, converted the barn and built the magnificent swimming pool himself. They have done 2 seasons so far.

We bought the property with a *chambres d'hôtes* in mind. We think we bought the right property, given the amount of money we had. Our criteria were that we had to have somewhere habitable but large enough to develop into at least 6 bedrooms. So we bought a house we could live in, with a barn completely in its original state. It took us about 2 years to get it into a condition where we could start taking paying guests. We've done a lot of renovation as the barn needed total redoing, the grounds needed doing, the swimming pool needed to be built, and we've actually done it all ourselves. Whether it was the best thing or not, we're not sure, but it was dictated by the amount of money we had to spend. We didn't have any major problems with the building work. We actually bought the property with planning permission to turn the barn into a dwelling, although we did change the plans substantially. It was intended to be 3 *gîtes*, and we turned it into a 6 bedroomed barn with large dining and games area. We haven't had any problems with officialdom, mainly because our mayor lives up the road and has been very helpful, just given us the nod and the wink really, and letting us know when we need to do something official.

We knew we wanted to move to France, but we had some years before we could receive a pension and so we obviously had to do something that produced an income, and we thought that a *chambres d'hôtes* would be a nice thing to do a) because it's seasonal and you're not working flat out the whole year, and b) because most people come on holiday to enjoy themselves. We thought the people that would come to this area of France for a holiday would be of like mind with us. And it's proved to be so. We get on with the French quite well; so far everybody has been extremely friendly and helpful. But the difficulty with the language means you are always communicating on a superficial level and it precludes developing any deeper friendships. Our guests are mainly British, that's because we advertise in English journals though we have had people from all other parts of Europe. Now we're in the *Gîtes de France* book we hope that will increase. So far all our guests have been really nice, all different obviously and sometimes we, as the owners, have to use quite a lot of tact because there are different people sitting round one table and you have to be the animator and make sure things go well.

In winter we tend to be fairly busy continuing to develop the place and maintaining the property. We do manage to take a break in November and February. We go to the UK about once a year but might not choose that if we didn't have family to visit. Getting up to do breakfasts is not too bad in the summer because it's usually beautiful mornings, apart from when you've had a very late night before. We all enjoy cooking and we try to use fresh local produce. We use mainly French recipes, but where we feel British recipes have something to add, then we use them. When guests arrive we try, the 3 of us, to be around to introduce ourselves and they are offered a drink: tea, coffee, cold drink, whatever; and the are given a very brief introduction to the place before being shown their rooms. We try not to overpower them because they have usually had a fairly long drive and are tired.

The housekeeping, the cleaning, and the laundry and stuff aren't too bad when the weather's good, as it usually is, but when we have wet weather, that can be a problem. Keeping up the grounds, the pool, and the general maintenance isn't particularly onerous, but it does have to be looked after every day. The most time-consuming thing is watering the plants. We like to have quite a few flowers around, and because it's such a dry time of year, everything needs watering every day and we spend a good hour and a half/two hours just watering. The administration, again, isn't particularly onerous because you're always around to take bookings, answer the phone etc., and the internet makes it much easier. You have to make sure the internet and the answerphone are attended if you're away, so that can be a problem. For advertising, we'll be in the *Gîtes de France* book for the first time this year, we're also in *Bonnes Vacances* which is very good, and we've got our own web site. When we give up the *chambres d'hôtes*, we'll be visiting the rest of France we haven't had time to visit so far.

Sally

Sally and her husband bought their house in 1998. It is in the country, and is a former farmhouse and barn, now converted into one house. They have three guest bedrooms which share one bathroom, and no other rooms specifically reserved for guests. They have a pleasant garden with a swimming pool.

We came to France four years ago and intended to run a *chambres d'hôtes*. We wanted to come out here to enjoy the country and grow our own fruit and vegetables. We wish we had bought a property where all the bedrooms had an en-suite. But we only have one shared bathroom for the guests so we've tried to keep it so it's one family at a time. If someone rings up and wants to come and there's someone here already I tell them that the bathroom is shared, so that they can decide. I also ask the people who are here if they mind sharing. Most people don't mind.

I had some French before we came, my husband none at all. During the first year we decided to saturate ourselves in French classes. We went to classes on Monday and Friday mornings, to a conversation group on Monday afternoons, and a different lesson on Wednesday mornings.

The house we bought was completely renovated and completely furnished, but it had been a second home only used in the summer. The windows aren't really good enough for the winter as we're on the top of a hill and it's very windy. The only thing we had to do immediately was to have a new septic tank as the previous one backed up into the downstairs bath. We found a French gentleman to do that and he was very helpful.

We're not doing the *chambres d'hôtes* on any large scale, we don't want to make our fortunes, but it does help our income. Our guests are mainly English people and we have had some New Zealanders. We don't advertise at all, it's mainly word of mouth because we've got a lot of friends, also the restaurant sends us some people, and another *chambres d'hôtes* nearby. And the people mostly come back, one couple is coming soon for the third time. We don't really want people dropping in off the streets, and we prefer them to stay for a week or ten days rather than one night. We don't use a computer.

This winter January and February were very busy, but normally we get the house ready for the next season and prepare the garden. We try to get home about three times a year to see ageing relatives – in the winter, mainly, when ferries are cheaper.

I don't mind cooking dinners, not that we do it as a regular thing. We offer guests dinner on their first night and they eat with us. After that I'm quite glad if they go to the local restaurant.

When we give up the *chambres d'hôtes* we won't be staying in this house because it'll be too large for us and the garden will be too big, but that'll only be when we are too old and grey to do it any longer.

Maggie

Maggie and her husband bought their house in 2002 and are so new to the B&B business that they haven't yet received their first guest. Their house is in the country, but only a 10-minute drive to a town with one of the country's landmark historic abbeys. It is a farmhouse that had been renovated by the former owners to the highest standard I have ever seen, and with grounds and swimming pool to match. They will have a small *gîte* and 3 letting bedrooms all with an en-suite, but no other rooms specifically reserved for guests.

It's a beautiful house in a beautiful setting. We had considered doing the same thing in England, but the weather's not so good. We think we bought the right property because it's even better placed than we anticipated before moving in. The problem really is French; I am going to French classes twice a week. We decided to run a *chambres d'hôtes* because we've taken early retirement and we like meeting people.

It's not ideal for children; we'll probably accept children over 10 but might have to change our ideas. It's definitely a bit windier than we thought and there's snow as well, but not consistently horrible like it is in the UK. We've been back to the UK once. I wondered if I would feel strange about coming back to France, but no, the joy of driving down an empty road and seeing the wonderful views made up for any qualms about leaving my sister and friends behind.

When we're up and running with the *chambres d'hôtes*, I would offer dinner by arrangement, probably 3 times a week, certainly on a Monday when things are closed, but I might change my mind and do more dinners. Breakfasts would be French style, I don't think there's any requirement to do the old English breakfast out here. The large garden was one of the reasons for buying the house, and, if the weather's hot, hopefully the plants won't grow too much. Probably one thing that would be tricky would be answering the phone initially, because I won't know if it's French people. If it is, then I have to struggle with the language a bit. We actually don't pay French tax at the moment, but we're going to sort it out because it would be beneficial for us to pay French tax rather than English. We've already sorted out our social security and we're awaiting our *Cartes de Séjour*. Amazingly, you're told that French bureaucracy is difficult; we just walked in and walked out; much easier than doing anything in the UK really.

We haven't decided where to advertise yet, but we're hoping to pick up bookings through the internet. My daughter-in-law is going to do us a web site. I'm going to have some printed literature done and take it to estate agents, and then we'll register with *Gîtes de France* because that's the only way the tourist office will accept us. One or two people have given me ideas of companies to advertise with that won't cost too much, because we're a small concern and haven't got that many rooms to let out. I really hope it works out because I'm getting quite excited about it all now. It's a big learning curve and any assistance from people locally on what to do and how to go about it is always welcomed. Hopefully, this time next year we'll be able to say, 'Oh look, we've got several people booked already, and repeats from last year'. So I wish us luck, even though I shouldn't say it myself.

TIPS FOR MAKING IT PAY

- ◆ Be there when guests arrive, personally take them to their room, and offer a welcoming drink.

- ◆ Take up references on anyone you employ; a mistake could be costly.

- ◆ Don't wear yourself out by doing it all yourself.

TIP FOR IMPROVING YOUR FRENCH

- ◆ Always reply in French to French people, even when they try to help you out in English.

14

The Customers

Who are they, these people who come as strangers and leave as friends?

NATIONALITY

This depends partly on your location and partly on where you advertise. If situated near the channel ports, you will receive mostly British people. In fact some of these B&Bs find their clientele is almost exclusively British through no particular desire on their part, just a result of proximity to the ports. Others set out deliberately to have only British guests and I personally think this is a mistake. The French guests that do arrive will not like being entirely surrounded by the English language, and I think the British guests are losing out too, because surely they haven't come to France just to meet their own kind. I strongly recommend you to give a warm welcome to all the world; it's much more interesting for all concerned. Anyway, one tends to have preconceived notions about nationality before people arrive. So many are on the move these days: we had British living in Spain, France, Czechoslovakia; Australians in Hong Kong, France, UK; the world's a real *pot-pourri* these days. Yet they were all taking a holiday in France.

We achieved:	Another British B&B:	National Average:
40% French	60% French	75% French
30% British	20% British	25% Rest
10% Benelux	20% Rest	
20% Rest		

You will see we did our very best to make the French welcome, but still got the backhanded compliment in our visitors' book from a military gentleman that we were 'a little bit of England in a French zone'. Owners will always have proportionally more of their own nationality because, of course, that's where they advertise. Proprietors near the top attractions such as Chartres, Avignon, etc, will have more Americans. The Japanese visit France in considerable numbers but usually in organized groups which do not use B&Bs. The Germans also are not great frequenters of B&Bs.

From the rest of the world you will only get an occasional visit, unless you have a special connection. The up-and-coming countries are believed to be in eastern Europe. We were taken aback one day when an expensive sports car drew up and the owner explained he was from Lithuania 'next to Russia'. Regretfully, he doesn't feature in our visitors' book as we were full. Have you any ideas for being ahead of the pack and cultivating their custom?

AGE

Staying in a *chambres d'hôtes* is very much the holiday choice for the 45 to 65 age group, so a lot of the customers are near retiring, early retired or already retired and you must bear this in mind when setting up your establishment. The next group is couples with babies and young children. There will be hardly any teenagers unless they happen to be en route to somewhere else. Young adults will only come if there is a sporting facility. Then there are a few quite frail elderly people; our oldest was 95.

HOLIDAYS

You will be disappointed to find that people **do not** come and stay for nice neat periods for a fortnight's holiday, Saturday to Saturday. Certainly, the majority of guests will be on holiday, but this has many variations. If you are in the country, or near the sea or mountains, then you will get the long-stay holiday customers, though people are restless these days and not many stay for a fortnight; a week is more usual. Just very exceptionally, there are those who stay three weeks, especially, with children. Far more common is a 2- to 4-night stay, and these are the people most likely to come back again and again. But for 75 per cent of B&Bs, the **mainstay of the business is one-night guests**.

FRENCH NAME	ENGLISH NAME	DATE	COMMENTS
Jour de l'An	New Year's Day	1st Jan	Public holiday
Jour des Rois	Twelfth Night	6th Jan	—
Mardi-Gras	Shrove Tuesday	Feb/Mar	—
Le 1 Avril	All Fools' Day	1st April	—
Vendredi Saint	Good Friday	Mar/Apr	Not a holiday
Pâques	Easter	Mar/Apr	Sunday
Pâques	Easter Monday	Mar/Apr	Public holiday
Fête du Travail	May Bank Holiday	1st May	Public holiday
Victoire 1945	VE Day	8th May	Public holiday
Ascension	Ascension Day	Varies	Public holiday
Pentecôte	Whitsun	Varies	Public holiday on Monday after
Fête Nationale	—	14th July	Public holiday
Assomption	Feast of the Assumption	15th August	Public holiday
Rentrée	Start of School Year	1st week in September	—
Halloween	Halloween	31st October	—
Toussaint	All Saint's Day	1st November	Public holiday
Armistice 1918	Remembrance Day	11th November	Public holiday
—	Christmas Eve	—	Not celebrated
Noël	Christmas Day	25th December	Public Holiday
—	Boxing Day	—	Not celebrated
Fête Ste Sylvestre	New Year's Eve	31st December	—

Figure 35   The French Year

OTHER REASONS FOR COMING

You will be amazed at all the other reasons why people are staying with you. The two most frequent with us were house hunting and attending a wedding. But there were many others: first communion, house warming, golden wedding, visiting sick relative, funeral, and of course many people didn't say. The house hunting group would be better described as 'property generally' because it also encompassed: selling, moving in or out, or keeping an eye on the building work. To give an idea of numbers, we can name 22 couples who stayed with us in connection with a property they own locally, and a great many more who were 'just looking'. It's a great source of out-of-season business.

People attending weddings were concentrated in the high season, especially the Saturdays nearest the 14th July and 15th August holidays. We had 3 or 4 groups a year, mostly French, but some British. Getting married in the country is quite the thing for the French, and for Brits too it's fashionable to marry in France, if there are parents living there to do the honours. The tourist office often provided the names of all the local hostelries for the wedding organiser to send out to the guests for them to make their choice. However some B&Bs are not thrilled by wedding guests in high season as they seldom have dinner, and most only stay for the Saturday night.

You may be hoping to fill the rooms out of season with business people, commercial travellers, and the like. I'm afraid not. Certainly you'll get a few, especially if you are in a village, but they mostly prefer somewhere with a bar. One could wish for more of them, but they are a difficult group to reach. How are you going to advertise to them? You may be lucky enough to find the occasional person working locally who needs temporary lodgings in the winter, perhaps for a week, perhaps three months. But they will want a **very** reduced price, out of which you have got to provide heating, and would need to discuss carefully what meals they want.

WHEN DO THEY COME?

These days a fortnight's stay in one place is rare, especially in a B&B, but most people now take several holidays a year. One of the prime reasons for having an international clientele is to try and lengthen the season; however, out-of-season stays are mostly only a couple of days.

The French are totally wedded to the 6 weeks comprising the second half of July and August. There is an old chestnut of a story in which a couple pretended to be away in August by shutting themselves in for the month, when actually they couldn't afford to go away. A Frenchman said to us, 'Now I am retired I can take my holiday early'. He meant the first week of July. Even for the French the last week of August is not so popular for couples with children because there is a long list of equipment for school that has to be purchased, and the list is not issued earlier. You will receive some custom for weekends and half terms and this is a very good reason for encouraging a French clientele.

The Scandinavians, Dutch and Belgians start their school summer holiday earlier than France or Britain, so they are likely to come at the beginning of July.

Unfortunately, many British couples without children still go away in the school holidays, either because they work in education, or they used to and don't want to change, or they like to holiday at the same time as grandchildren. The British and American 'slightly older' couples favour September.

Until recently, foreigners only came for weekends and half-terms to areas near their own country. Now the introduction of cheap flights to provincial airports has made short-stay and out-of-season trips feasible much further afield. But short breaks are still only popular for the mid-season periods; it's all but impossible to do much in the winter, except for skiing.

THE WELCOME (*L'Accueil*)

The French set great store by the welcome they receive on arrival. It is mentioned over and over again in the literature on *chambres d'hôtes*. This puzzled me for a long time, because **of course** the guests will be made welcome with a big smile, a handshake, being shown personally to their room, and then sat down with a cup of tea or coffee. What else? A proprietor is in business to make a living, if the guests don't like the welcome they might leave and certainly won't come again. I asked a French friend for an explanation and was told that in a hotel you are given a key by a po faced receptionist and told to find the room yourself, at least anywhere less than 5 stars. The fact is, it is in the French nature to be cautious and it's revealing that their word *étranger* means 'outsider' or 'stranger' as well as 'foreigner'. They feel you cannot know if an *étranger* is to be trusted, so it's better to keep your distance. To smile straight away is superficial, much later on it will mean something.

Therefore a *chambres d'hôtes* proprietor has got to be un-French to a remarkable degree. To us and the Americans it's second nature to smile and be pleasant. We are taught that from an early age, so we can't see the problem. Nevertheless, do be a bit careful with the welcome, it is just possible they have come for a funeral. In fact be guided by the customer as to how friendly and chatty they want to be. Don't be intrusive but let people know where to find you if they need any help.

ETIQUETTE

This is always a problem in another country. As a visitor you will be forgiven much, but in business you are expected to know. In France you **must** use the local manners. The first thing is to shake hands with everyone as soon as they arrive. And I mean **everyone**; it is impolite to leave anyone out, even children, though for children under 5 you could ask their name by way of a greeting. Say *bonjour* to everyone the first time you meet them every day. But it is not polite to say it again because that means you have forgotten the earlier meeting.

During the day at least one of the patrons should try and say some pleasantry to each guest. First names are not used nearly as much as we do; you would need to know the guest well, but modify this according to age of guest. In fact, on the first greeting, you should not even use the surname, it's *bonjour, madame/monsieur*. After about 6pm it's *bonsoir* and this means 'hello' as well as 'goodbye'. After a couple of days you could add to your *bonjour* the words *ça va?* which means literally 'how goes it?'. The other will probably reply *ça va*. It's just like the English 'how do you do', where the reply is not expected to be full details of your latest operation.

A particular difficulty for Anglophones is the use of the second person singular which has totally disappeared from our everyday language. It **must** be used to children under about 10, to animals, and when speaking to your spouse. Since it needs a completely different set of verb endings it needs some nimble thinking. Use the word *madame* to all women over about 18; it doesn't have the connotation of being married any more than the English use of Mr to all males.

When people leave, you do the hand-shaking routine all over again, but this time a young child may raise it's head for a kiss, in which case go ahead. Otherwise you do not kiss the paying guests. From the B&B viewpoint, the French are so good at departures. They load up the car and the **very last thing** is for them all to come and say goodbye. Then you know they've gone and you can go and do their room. The British are so wishy-washy, they can drift about for half an hour saying goodbye, or sometimes they don't bother. If you've got to shake everyone's hand, then they will expect to reciprocate, and all the patrons should try and be present at departures, though it's not always possible. Then when we waved them off as they went down the drive it was like continually saying goodbye to friends; actually it's a bit wearing by the end of the season because it could add up to 500 people.

When foreigners choose to stay in a *chambres d'hôtes* in France, they will expect to encounter the French way of life, so it's not necessary to modify your approach to each, though sometimes they will look puzzled by your outstretched hand.

In everyday speech and on the phone, your French will sound very stilted because you lack all the little interjections. Try some of the following:

oui=bien sûr (certainly)
  d'accord (agreed)
  pas de problème (no problem)
  ah bon (oh good)
  tout à fait (quite so)
  pas de tout (not at all)
  avec plaisir (with pleasure)
  parfait (splendid, perfect)

non=je regrette (I'm sorry)
  désolé (extremely sorry)
  impossible (impossible)

CHILDREN

The possibilities are:

1. Be as child-friendly as possible.

2. Do nothing special and you won't get many.

3. Don't allow children at all: difficult if you accept one night stays, and anyway it's illegal.

In fact, you don't get that many British children as it's not a holiday type that has ever been marketed specially for them. This is fortunate perhaps, as they are so badly behaved, or am I being too censorious of my compatriots? The children we had were mostly French and Belgian and on a wet day they were sat down at the dining-table by their parents to do extra homework without evident complaint. We noticed that parents often expected to find other children for theirs to play with, but it was most unlikely for there to be any of the same age.

Children are a great responsibility, and you must do your best with safety precautions so that you won't be criticised if there is an accident. Also, of course you're expected to have a very reduced price for children, and even be totally free for babies. Children need a lot of equipment to keep them amused, they break things, they lose things, they're noisy, they are a nuisance at table, and they wet the bed. But in spite of all those things, they're a joy to have around and we did as much as possible to encourage families.

Babies

You need a cot and high-chair even though many parents bring their own. We expected parents to bring their own baby food which we would heat in our microwave. This is where a kitchenette for the guests is most convenient, otherwise parents are likely to invade your kitchen at any time of the day. We only had 2 or 3 babies a year, and there were never any complaints about them crying, or were the other guests being polite?

Toddlers

They are much more of a problem and their safety is a worry. We didn't have a gate at the top of the stairs as I couldn't see other guests remembering to shut it. Maybe we should have. Ornaments need lifting above child head height. Parents generally bring plenty of toys, so don't provide much, and certainly not books which won't last 5 minutes. On no account take on baby sitting or child-minding. Explain that you are not insured for this.

5–12 Years

Older children need occupying and this is where most of your equipment should be directed. They will monopolise the pool of course, and will be prime users of everything else. They will also poke into places where they shouldn't, so all stores should be locked. They need amusing indoors too – the TV of course, also board games, cards, table-football, table tennis, whatever you can provide. Unless you are actively watching children in some activity, **do not** let the parents expect you to keep an eye on them while you are working. A horror story I heard was that the parents went for a walk, leaving the children to play in the garden. Well, those children cut off the cat's whiskers and rode on the dog such that its back was injured and it had to be put down.

Teenagers

French teenagers holiday with their parents longer than other nationalities, but it is quite beyond your scope to provide for them. Just direct them to your brochure display stand where they will find info. on riding stables, quad cars, championship size swimming pool, tennis courts, etc. They eat a lot too, except girls who are slimming.

DISABLED AND ELDERLY CUSTOMERS

Some of our customers were very frail looking, and that was a worry too. Well, it's their choice if they're still travelling, but when I saw them trying to park, I did wish they weren't still driving. Elderly people usually have small appetites and would appreciate a reduced meal.

A bathroom for the disabled does look a bit institutional, but the facilities are also appreciated by couples with a baby. And bear in mind that some people are temporarily disabled, for example by having a leg in plaster.

Naturally you should not refuse to take the very occasional mentally handicapped person. Your attitude will influence the other guests' reaction. Remove small objects from the room, and if meals look like being a problem suggest a different time.

CUSTOMERS' PETS

Mainland Europeans have always liked to bring their dogs and cats on holiday. I am sure that Brits will too, more and more now that it is possible. Do you want them? We stated that we did not accept animals, but occasionally could be persuaded. At least then we could refuse if we wanted to. Although people don't like extras, I would make a charge for animals so that you've got some recompense for the 1 in 10 that will do some damage. If you don't take animals, what will you do about the people who forgot to mention they had one? Just sigh, accept them, and charge.

CUSTOMERS YOU COULD DO WITHOUT

Fortunately few, but you will get one or two. Prize bores at the table were one of the lesser hazards. For complaints the golden rule is to respond immediately. Unfortunately the aggro usually flares up when more than one thing has gone wrong. Sometimes it is your fault, sometimes theirs, but it all adds up to an unpleasant explosion. Hold you temper; don't make excuses – they only sound lame. Then do your utmost to put right whatever is wrong **immediately**, though sometimes this is impossible. The plumber or electrician won't come in under 24 hours; the spare part needs ordering. Only offer a refund as a last resort; better to offer a good bottle of wine. Keep the discussion away from other guests or it will upset them too. Don't take it to heart; it happens to all proprietors sooner or later.

TOURIST INFORMATION

You are expected to be a fount of local knowledge. It's all part of the service to advise the clients on their itineraries, shopping, restaurants, sports facilities and where to buy organic walnut oil.

Once you feature in the B&B guides, you will be inundated with tourist literature, and just laid out on a table it will need tidying every day. It was a great help when we bought a proper set of display stands. It's a good idea to have a large pin-up board for the posters of forthcoming events, and it can take other information like church services/list of markets/names of doctor, dentist, chemist, optician. And you may like to put up cards from restaurants, taxis, garage, hairdressers – all those useful people. Prominently display information on local vineyards; it's what many people come to France for.

In particular you should carry information on all the local sports facilities, though I have to admit that ten-pin bowling had us stumped once (the guest did find some). Ask the tourist office if they have a book of *petites randonnées* (walks); also ask where to obtain fishing permits and a map of areas available. There is a *carte de pêche vacance* valid for 15 consecutive days between 1st June and 30th Sep, or a daily card.

A good idea is to mount a series of maps showing the local walks, and some day or half-day circuits for car excursions. Mount them on card and have them plasticised by a printing firm. You'll lose one or two a year but they are very popular.

The emergency number is **not** 999, so a list should be attached to the telephone:

SAMU (ambulance)	15
Police	17
Pompiers (fire)	18
English speaking emergency	112 (all services)

STRANGERS IN A FOREIGN LAND

Sometimes the help guests ask for goes well beyond the standard queries. Be a little cautious; it can take up a lot of time, and if it's medical, you may not be the right person to help. By all means give local lifts as a good will gesture, but do not ferry people to airports, stations, etc. You are not insured to take passengers and you don't know how much to charge. If they are in a fix, they'll just have to take a taxi. EU nationals may ask for help in claiming their medical refunds from the French system. Tell them it is possible to get the money straight away if they go in person to the *CPAM* office, otherwise they'll get a cheque in euros back home.

Very few of your guests will have absolutely no French or English. I can only remember 3 jolly Italian taxi drivers (visiting France for a dog show, of course), and an Argentinian family. But this is not to say they can all converse fluently and they too will have difficulties on the phone. They may ask you to make a reservation at a restaurant, or book their next night's stay. Take this on just to be helpful. For most guests, language didn't seem to matter as long as people were friendly. We felt it was only the Brits who worried about a 'language problem'.

THE END OF THE DAY

Until my children were well into their teens, I used to look in on them before going to bed, just to check they were all right. Obviously I didn't look into the guests' bedrooms, but as I went round the house a little before midnight, locking the outside doors, closing windows and turning off lights, it did seem as if I was checking that all was well with the people in my charge again.

TIPS FOR MAKING IT PAY

◆ Aim for a worldwide clientele to lengthen the season.

◆ Deal with complaints promptly and give a free bottle of wine, not a discount.

TIP FOR IMPROVING YOUR FRENCH

◆ *Lisez un roman en français.*

Postscript

Having read this far I assume you are seriously contemplating a life across the Channel and it seems appropriate to include a final few words of encouragement about France and the French.

Firstly it is, like Britain, a settled, cultured land with all the services you would expect, where freedom of speech, movement and published opinion are guaranteed under the law. In short it is a modern democratic society.

As for the French themselves, there is a persistent myth that they are unfriendly, difficult and somehow unacceptably idiosyncratic. All nations have characteristics peculiar to their society, including the British of course. '*Vive la différence*', as the French themselves would say. Don't waste time making unfavourable comparisons, as if Britain was a repository of all the virtues. It isn't, and we can learn something from the French, for example their concern for family values and quality of life.

Personal difficulties spring mostly from misunderstandings or misconceptions. If offence is caused either way, and it will happen sometimes, well that's life. It could happen anywhere in the world.

Our own experience has been overwhelmingly positive. We have been accepted with genuine warmth and friendliness and have no regrets in adapting to the French way of life.

By meeting the French half way and making yourself aware of their social code without prejudice or preconceptions, you are embarking on an enriching experience.

Le dernier qui quittera l'Angleterre est prié d'éteindre la lumière

Appendix A – Les Plus Beaux Villages de France

Alsace
Bas-Rhin
  Hunspach
  Mittelbergheim
Haut-Rhin
  Hunawihr
  Riquewihr

Aquitaine
Dordogne
  Belvès
  Beynac-et-Cazenac
  Domme
  Limeuil
  Monpazier
  La Roque-Gageac
  Saint-Jean-de-Côle
  Saint-Léon-sur-Vézère
Lot-et-Garonne
  Monflanquin
  Pujols-le-Haut
Pyrénées-Atlantiques
  Aînhoa
  La Bastide-Clairance
  Sare

Auvergne
Allier
  Charroux
Cantal

Salers
Tournemire
Haute-Loire
  Arlempdes
  Blesle
  Lavaudieu
  Pradelles
Puy-de-Dôme
  Montpeyroux
  Saint-Floret
  Saint-Sarurnin
  Usson

Basse-Normandie
Calvados
  Beuvron-en-Auge
Manche
  Barfleur
Orne
  Saint-Céneru-le-Gérei

Bourgogne
Côte-d'Or
  Châteauneuf
  Flavigny-sur-Ozerain
Saône-et-Loire
  Semur-en-Brionnais
Yonne
  Noyers-sur-Serein
  Vézelay

Bretagne
Finistère
   La Faou
   Île-de-Sein
   Locronan
Ille-et-Vilaine
   Saint-Suliac

Centre
Cher
   Apremont-sur-Allier
Indre
   Gargilesse-Dampierre
   Saint-Benoit-du-Sault
Indre-et-Loire
   Candes-Saint-Martin
   Crissy-sur-Manse
   Montrésor
Loir-et-Cher
   Lavardin
Loiret
   Yèvre-le Châtel

Corse
Corse-du-Sud
   Piana
Haute-Corse
   Sant'Antonino

Franche-Comté
Doubs
   Lods
Haute-Saône
   Pesmes
Jura
   Baume-Les-Messieurs
   Château-Chalon

Haute-Normandie
Eure
   Lyons-la-Forêt

Ile-de-France
Val-d'Oise
   La Roche-Guyon

Langedoc-Roussillon
Aude
   Lagrasse
Hérault
   Minerve
   Olargues
   Saint-Guilhem-le-Désert
Lozère
   La Garde-Guérin
   Saint-Enimie
Pyrénées-Orientales
   Castelnou
   Eus
   Mosset
   Villefranche-le-Conflent

Limousin
Corrèze
   Collognes-la-Rouge
   Curemonte
   Saint-Robert
   Ségur-le-Château
   Treignac-sur-Vézère
   Turenne
Haute-Vienne
   Mortmart

Lorraine
Moselle
   Rodemack

Saint-Querin

Midi-Pyrénées
Ariège
  Camon
  Saint-Lizier
Aveyron
  Belcastel
  Brousse'le-Château
  Conques
  La Couvertoirade
  Estaing
  Najac
  Saint-Côme-d'Olt
  Sainte-Eulalie-d'Olt
  Sauveterre-de-Rouergue
Gers
  Larressingle
  Montréal-du-Gers
  Sarrant
Haute-Garonne
  Saint-Bertrand-de-Cominges
Lot
  Autoire
  Cardaillac
  Carennac
  Lacapelle-Marival
  Loubressac
  Saint-Cirq-Lapopie
Tarn
  Corrze Castelnau-de-Montmiral
  Lautrec
  Monestiés
  Puycelsi-Grésigne
Tarn-et-Garonne
  Auvillar
  Bruniquel

Lauzerte

Pays De La Loire
Maine-et-Loire
  Montsoreau
Vendée
  Vouvant

Picardie
Aisne
  Parfondeval
Oise
  Gerberoy

Poitou-Charantes
Charente
  Aubeterre-sur-Dronne
Charante-Maritime
  Ars-en-Ré
  La Flotte-en-Ré
  Mornac-sur-Seudre
  Talmont-sur-Gironde
Deux-Sèvres
  Coulon
Vienne
  Angles-sur-l'Anglin

Provence-Alpes-Côte d'Azur
Alpes-de-Haute-Provence
  Moustiers-Sainte-Marie
Alpes-Maritimes
  Coaraze
  Gourdon
  Saint-Agnès
Bouches-du-Rhône
  Les Beaux-de-Provence
Hautes-Alpes
  La-Grave-la-Meije

Saint-Véran
Var
  Bargème
  Gassin
  Seillans
  Tourtour
Vaucluse
  Ansouis
  Gordes
  Lourmarin
  Ménerbes
  Roussillon
  Séguret
  Venasque

Rhône-Alpes
Ain
  Pérouges
Ardèche
  Balazuc
  Vogüé

Drôme
  La Garde-Adhémar
  Mirmande
  Montbrun-les-Bains
  Le Poët-Laval
Loire
  Sainte-Croix-en-Jarez
Savoie
  Bonneval-sur-Arc
Haute-Savoie
  Sixt-Fer-à-Cheval
  Yvoire

Dom-Tom
La Runion
Hell-Bourg

Appendix B – Useful Books

If any of these titles are out of print they can be requested from a public library.

These are in English:
Buying and Restoring Old Property in France, David Everett (Robert Hale)
Buying A Property In France, Clive Kristen (How To Books)
The Food of France, Waverley Root (Macmillan)
Foolproof French Cooking, Raymond Blanc (BBB Worldwide Ltd)
The French Country Garden, Louisa Jones (Thames and Hudson)
French or Foe?, Polly Platt (Culture Crossings Ltd)
    An American looks at life and business in France
Going to Live in France, Alan Hart (How To Books)
The French Room, Elizabeth Wilhide (Conran Octopus)
Jenny Baker's Cuisine Grandmére, Jenny Baker (Faber and Faber)
Living in France, Bill Blevins and David Franks (Blackstone Franks)
Mrs Beeton's Book Of Household Management, Isabella Beeton (Facsimile Edition – Chancellor Press)
    For the household management, not the recipes
Pétanque: French Game of Boules, Garth Freeman (Carreau Press)
Recipes From Quercy, Claudine Duluat and Jeanine Pouget (Les Editions Du Laquet)
Simple French Cuisine, Jenny Baker (Faber and Faber)
The Traveller's French Food & Drink Dictionary, Robyn Wilson (Warner Books)
The Ultimate Pool Maintenance Manual, Terry Tamminen (McGraw Hill Education)
Well Preserved: A Jam Making Hymnal, Joan Hassol (Prentice Hall & IBD)

These are in French:

Crumbles, Camille Le Foll (Marabout Ct Cuisine)
   Yes truly, this is a French cook book, and the recipes will be a great talking point at the table
La Cuisine Facile d'Aujourd'hui, Delia Smith (Hachette)
   A selection of her recipes translated into French
Les Plus Beaux Villages de France, Sélection du Reader's Digest

Appendix C – Useful Addresses

Always drop the first '0' when telephoning from another country. Numbers beginning with '08' cannot be dialled from another country.

Architects

(Registered in France and English-speaking.)

Raymond Burton, Vitarel, 82110 Montagudet, Tarn et Garonne, France.
  Tel: 05 63 94 60 26
  Email: burton.raymond@wanadoo.fr

Vladimir Katelbach, 3 rue Ernest Jeanbernat, 31000 Toulouse, France.
  Tel: 05 61 99 65 13
  Email: vlakatel@club-internet.fr

Robert Lyell, 4 Alle des Maronniers, 11300 Limoux, Aude, France.
  Tel: 04 68 31 25 66
  Email: roblyell.arch@tiscali.fr

Iain Stewart, 8 rue Pailleron, 69004 Lyon, France.
  Tel: 04 78 30 01 92
  Email: istewart@club.internet.fr
  Web: www.architect.fr

Pierre Weingaertner, Le Mas des Coustes, Route de St Canadet, 13100 Aix en Provence, France.
  Tel: 06 60 55 29 74
  Email: expert-surveyor@wanadoo.fr

British Officialdom

British Embassy, 35 rue de Faubourg St Honoré, 75008 Paris, France.
  Tel: 01 44 51 31 02

Department of Social Security, Overseas Benefits Directorate (Med), Longbenton, Newcastle on Tyne NE98 1YX.
  (For National Health)

Inland Revenue National Insurance Contributions Office, Longbenton,
Newcastle on Tyne NE98 1ZZ.
Tel: 0191 225 5811
(For pensions)

Cookery course

Leiths School of Food & Wine, 21 St Albans Grove, London W1 5BP.
Tel: 020 7229 0177
Email: info@leiths.com
Web: www.leiths.com

Estate agents

These agents make a special point of selling B&Bs as a going concern.
Currie French Properties, 2 Fulbrooke Road, Cambridge CB3 9EE.
Tel: 01223 576084
Email: cfps@ntlworld.com
Web: www.french-property.com/currie
Links French Property Service Ltd, Les Claudits, 36160 Vijon, France.
Tel: 02 54 30 57 92
Email: linksfrenchproperty@wanadoo.fr
Web: www.linksproperty.co.uk

Language courses

Alliance Française, 1 Dorset Square, London NW1 6PU.
Tel: 020 7224 1865
Web: www.alliancefrancaise.org.uk
Hotcourses
(Directory of full time, part time, evening, weekend, courses; searchable
by region and city)
Web: www.hotcourses.com
Open University, Walton Hall, Milton Keynes MK7 6AA.
Tel: 01908 659141
www/open.ac.uk

Magazines and newspapers

France, Digbeth Street, Stow On The Wold, Glos. GL54 1BN.
(For background information)

Tel: 01451 831398

Email: francemag@btinternet.com

French Property News, 6 Burgess Mews, London SW19 1UF.

(For property exhibitions and property for sale)

Tel: 020 8543 3113

Email: info@french-property-news.com

Web: www.french-property-news.com

The News, France.

(Gives help and information to new residents)

Tel:05 53 06 84 40

Email: editor@french-news.com

subs@french-news.com

Mail order

General catalogues

La Redoute, 59081 Roubaix Cedex 2, France.

Tel: 08 92 350 350

Web: www.laredoute.fr

3 Suisses, 59345 Croix Cedex.

Tel: 08 92 69 15 00

Web: www.3suisses.fr

Hotel Linen

Linvosges Hôtellerie, 6 place de la Gare, 88400 Gerardmer, France.

Tel: 08 92 68 88 03

Web: www.linvosges.com

Miscellaneous

BigDishSatellite, Mouriol, Milhaguet, 87440 Marvel, France.

(BT to FT telephone adaptors)

Tel: 05 55 78 72 98

Email: office@bigdishsat.com

Web: www.bigdishsat.com

Chèques-Vacances, 5 rue Gabriel Pri, 92584 Clichy Cedex, France.

Tel: 0891 670 570

Web: www.ancv.com

French Chamber of Commerce,21 Dartmouth St, London SW1H 9HP.
(Get their book *Setting Up A Business In France*)
Tel: 020 7304 4040

French Government Tourist Office, 178 Piccadilly, London W1V OAL.
Tel: 0171 491 7622

Piscines Waterair, ZA, 68580 Seppois-le-Bas, France.
(Steel lined swimming pools)
Tel: (in France) 0 825 00 05 58
Email: info@waterair.com
Web: www.waterair.com

St John's Supplies
(St John's Ambulance health and safety equipment)
Tel: 020 7278 7888
Email: C.Services@sjsupplies.demon.co.uk
Web: www.stjohnsupplies.co.uk

Index